Pasta

Classic and contemporary dishes for all pasta lovers

This edition published in 2011

LOVE FOOD is an imprint of Parragon Books Ltd

Parragon
Queen Street House
4 Queen Street
Bath BA1 1HE, UK

ISBN: 978-1-4454-5698-0

Printed in China

Photography by Don Last
Home Economy by Christiqne France
Introduction by Linda Doeser

Notes for the Reader
This book uses both metric and imperial measurements. Follow the same units of measurement throughout; do not mix metric and imperial. All spoon measurements are level: teaspoons are assumed to be 5 ml, and tablespoons are assumed to be 15 ml. Unless otherwise stated, milk is assumed to be full fat, eggs and individual vegetables are medium, and pepper is freshly ground black pepper.

The times given are an approximate guide only. Preparation times differ according to the techniques used by different people and the cooking times may also vary from those given. Optional ingredients, variations or serving suggestions have not been included in the calculations.

Recipes using raw or very lightly cooked eggs should be avoided by infants, the elderly, pregnant women, convalescents and anyone suffering from an illness. Pregnant and breastfeeding women are advised to avoid eating peanuts and peanut products. Sufferers from nut allergies should be aware that some of the ready-made ingredients used in the recipes in this book may contain nuts. Always check the packaging before use.

Vegetarians should be aware that some of the ready-made ingredients used in the recipes in this book may contain animal products. Always check the packaging before use.

CONTENTS

Introduction

Pasta is arguably the most useful ingredient to be found in any kitchen. It goes with just about anything else you can think of, from vegetables and cheese to meat and fish. It's equally delicious served with simple, inexpensive sauces or extravagant, luxurious mixtures, and it can be added to soups or form the basis of filling baked dishes. It may be a main meal, a first course dish or a delightfully different salad and because it's so versatile it's easy to find fabulous pasta recipes for all occasions and every season of the year. Virtually everyone loves pasta and it's especially popular with children. High in complex carbohydrates, it provides a steady release of energy but contains hardly any fat. Depending on the type of wheat flour used in its manufacture, it can also be a good source of protein, as well as B vitamins, potassium and iron. Moreover, it's economical, convenient and the dried variety keeps well. Huge numbers of pasta dishes can be prepared and cooked within 30 minutes and many take only half that time. Even making your own fresh pasta is quicker and easier than you may think – why not try and see for yourself? It is incredibly versatile and can be cut into ribbons, shaped or filled to create ravioli or tortellini.

There are hundreds of pasta shapes and new ones are being introduced all the time. There are no hard and fast rules about which shape goes with a particular sauce, although there are some traditional partnerships, such as Spaghetti Bolognese and Fettucine all'Alfredo. However, there are some useful guidelines. Long, thin pasta, such as spaghetti and linguine, is ideal for seafood sauces and light olive oil or fresh tomato dressings, but cannot really hold thick or chunky sauces. These are better served with pasta shapes that trap the sauce in hollows and ridges – penne (quills), fusilli (spirals) or conchiglie (shells), for example. Flat ribbons, such as tagliatelle, fettucine and pappardelle, are perfect for rich or creamy sauces. Baked dishes are often made with lasagne – flat sheets of pasta that can be layered with a variety of sauces – or cannelloni – tubes that can be filled and baked in a sauce. Smaller shapes, such as macaroni and rigatoni, are also often used in baking. Very small pasta shapes, such as stellete (stars) and anellini (rings) are used in soups, and filled pasta, such as ravioli and tortellini, is also served 'in broth'.

Making Fresh Pasta

For convenience, most of the recipes in this book use dried pasta. However, if you want to have a go at making filled pasta, such as ravioli, you will need to prepare the dough yourself. Making fresh pasta is not as difficult as you may believe and the same basic dough can also be used to make lasagne sheets and a variety of shapes, such as tagliatelle, pappardelle and macaroni. You won't need any special equipment (a pasta machine makes the job of rolling the dough simpler but it's not strictly necessary) and the process is both easy and satisfying.

Basic Pasta Dough

Serves 3–4

200 g/7 oz strong white bread flour,
  plus extra for dusting
pinch of salt
2 eggs, lightly beaten
1 tbsp olive oil

1 Sift together the flour and salt onto a work surface and make a well in the centre with your fingers. Pour the eggs and oil into the well, then using the fingers of one hand, gradually incorporate the flour into the liquid.

2 Knead the dough on a lightly floured work surface until it is completely smooth. Wrap in clingfilm and leave to rest for 30 minutes before rolling out or feeding through a pasta machine. Resting makes the dough more elastic.

Flavoured Pasta

The Basic Pasta Dough recipe may be flavoured and coloured by the addition of other ingredients.

Tomato pasta: Add 2 tablespoons of tomato purée to the well in the flour and use only 1½ eggs instead of 2.

Spinach pasta: Blanch 225 g/8 oz spinach in boiling water for 1 minute, then drain and squeeze out as much liquid as possible. Alternatively, use 150 g/5½ oz thawed frozen spinach. This does not need blanching, but as much liquid as possible should be squeezed out. Finely chop the spinach and mix with the flour before making a well and adding the eggs and oil.

Herb pasta: Add 3 tablespoons of finely chopped fresh herbs to the flour before making a well and adding the eggs and oil.

Wholemeal pasta: Use 140 g/5 oz wholemeal flour with 25 g/1 oz strong white bread flour and use 2 eggs.

Rolling Out Pasta Dough

When the fresh dough has rested, it may be rolled out by hand or with a pasta machine. Large quantities of dough should be halved or cut into quarters before rolling out. Keep covered until you are ready to work on them. To roll out by hand, lightly dust a work surface with plain flour, then roll out the pasta dough with a lightly floured rolling pin, always rolling away from you and turning the dough a quarter turn each time. Keep rolling to make a rectangle 2–3 mm/¹⁄₁₆–⅛ inch thick. The dough can then be cut into ribbons, stamped out with a biscuit cutter or filled and cut out to make ravioli.

A pasta machine makes rolling out the dough easier and quicker and ensures that it is even. There are a number of models available, the most useful being a hand-cranked machine with attachable cutters. An electric machine is even easier to use but somewhat extravagant. Cut the dough into manageable-sized pieces – 1 quantity Basic Pasta Dough should be cut into 4 pieces, for example. Flatten a piece with your hand and wrap the others in clingfilm until required. Fold the flat piece into thirds and feed it through the pasta machine on its widest setting. Repeat the folding and rolling 3 or 4 more times on this setting, then close the rollers by one notch. Continue feeding the dough through the rollers, without folding into thirds, gradually reducing the setting until you reach the narrowest. If you want to make ribbons, cut the dough into 30-cm/12-inch strips and feed through the appropriate cutter.

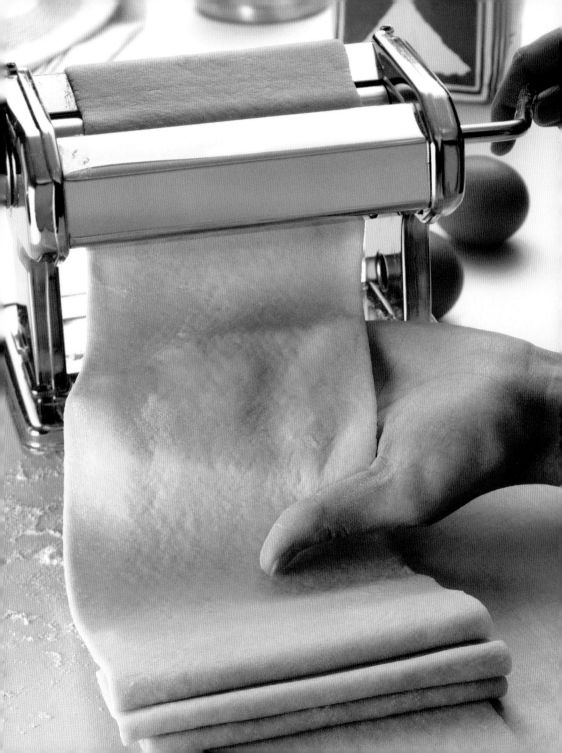

Cutting and Shaping Fresh Pasta

Pasta machines usually have a wide cutter for tagliatelle and a narrower one for tagliarini. Other pasta shapes can be cut by hand, as can hand-rolled pasta dough. To make pappardelle, use a serrated pastry wheel or pasta wheel to cut 2.5-cm/1-inch wide ribbons from the rolled out dough. To make tagliatelle or tagliarini, roll up a strip of dough like a Swiss roll and then cut into 5-mm/¼-inch (tagliatelle) or 3-mm/⅛-inch slices (tagliarini) with a sharp knife. To make macaroni, cut the pasta dough into 2.5-cm/1-inch squares with a sharp knife, then roll them corner to corner around a chopstick to form tubes. Slide off and let dry slightly.

Making Filled Pasta

Ravioli

Italians use the word ravioli as an all-purpose term for filled pasta and they can, therefore, be a variety of shapes.

Half-moon ravioli

1 Roll out the pasta dough to 2–3 mm/¹⁄₁₆–⅛ inch thick. Using a 5-cm/2-inch biscuit cutter, stamp out rounds.

2 Place about 1 teaspoon of the prepared filling in the centre of each round. Brush the edges of each round with a little water or beaten egg, then fold them in half to make half moons and press the edges to seal.

3 Place on a floured tea towel and let stand for 30–60 minutes to dry out slightly before cooking.

Ravioli rounds

1 Roll out the pasta dough to 2–3 mm/¹⁄₁₆–⅛ inch thick. Using a 5-cm/2-inch biscuit cutter, stamp out rounds.

2 Place 1 teaspoon of the filling on half of the rounds. Brush the edges with water or beaten egg, then cover with the remaining rounds, pressing the edges to seal.

3 Place on a floured tea towel and let stand for 30–60 minutes to dry out slightly before cooking.

Square ravioli

1 Divide the pasta dough in half and wrap 1 piece in clingfilm. Roll out the other piece to a rectangle 2–3 mm/¹⁄₁₆–⅛ inch thick. Cover with a damp tea towel and roll out the other piece of dough to the same size.

2 Place 1 teaspoon of the prepared filling in neat rows spaced about 4 cm/1½ inches apart on a sheet of pasta dough. Brush the spaces between the mounds with beaten egg or water.

3 Using a rolling pin, place the second sheet of dough on top and press down firmly between the pockets of filling, pushing out any air bubbles. Using a pasta wheel or sharp knife cut into squares. Place on a floured tea towel and let stand for 30–60 minutes to dry out slightly before cooking.

Tortellini

There are several legends about the origins of these pasta twists, the most famous of which being that they were inspired by the navel of Venus, goddess of love.

1 Roll out the pasta dough to 2–3 mm/¹⁄₁₆–⅛ inch thick. Using a 5-cm/2-inch plain biscuit cutter, stamp out rounds.

2 Place about 1 teaspoon of the prepared filling in the centre of each round. Brush the edges of each round with a little water or beaten egg, then fold them in half to make half moons and press the edges to seal.

3 Wrap a half moon around the tip of your index finger until the corners meet and press them together to seal. Repeat with the remaining pasta half moons. Place the filled tortellini on a floured dish towel and let stand for 30–60 minutes to dry out slightly before cooking.

Soups & Salads

Adding pasta to home-made soups not only makes them more substantial and filling, but also provides extra texture and interest. There are dozens of different tiny pasta shapes, all guaranteed to encourage children of all ages to finish every last drop in the bowl. Pasta salads are an easy and delicious way to add variety to the summer menu. As pasta goes so well with other ingredients, from cheese to chicken, you'll never be short of great ideas for an al fresco lunch or healthy side dish.

Minestrone Milanese

Heat the olive oil in a large, heavy-based saucepan. Add the pancetta, onions and garlic and cook, stirring occasionally, for 5 minutes. Add the carrots and celery and cook, stirring occasionally, for a further 5 minutes, or until all the vegetables are softened.

Drain the haricot beans and add them to the saucepan with the tomatoes and their can juices and the beef stock. Bring to the boil, reduce the heat, cover and simmer for 1 hour.

Add the potatoes, re-cover and cook for 15 minutes, then add the pasta, green beans, peas, cabbage and parsley. Cover and cook for a further 15 minutes, until all the vegetables are tender. Season to taste with salt and pepper. Ladle into warmed soup bowls and serve immediately with Parmesan cheese shavings.

SERVES 6

2 tbsp olive oil

55 g/2 oz rindless pancetta or streaky bacon, diced

2 onions, sliced

2 garlic cloves, finely chopped

3 carrots, chopped

2 celery sticks, chopped

225 g/8 oz haricot beans, soaked in cold water to cover for 3–4 hours

400 g/14 oz canned chopped tomatoes

2 litres/3½ pints beef stock

350 g/12 oz potatoes, diced

175 g/6 oz dried macaroni or other soup pasta shapes

175 g/6 oz green beans, sliced

115 g/4 oz fresh or frozen peas

225 g/8 oz Savoy cabbage, shredded

3 tbsp chopped fresh flat-leaf parsley

salt and pepper

fresh Parmesan cheese shavings, to serve

Tomato Broth with Angel Hair Pasta

Put the tomatoes, garlic cloves, onion, saffron, sugar, bouquet garni and lemon rind into a large, heavy-based saucepan. Pour in the stock and bring to the boil, then lower the heat, cover and simmer, stirring occasionally, for 25–30 minutes, until the tomatoes have disintegrated.

Remove the pan from the heat and leave to cool slightly. Remove and discard the garlic cloves, bouquet garni and lemon rind. Ladle the tomato mixture into a food processor or blender and process to a purée.

Return the purée to the rinsed-out pan and season to taste with salt and pepper. Stir in the olive oil and bring to the boil. Add the pasta, bring back to the boil and cook for 2–4 minutes, until tender but still firm to the bite.

Taste and adjust the seasoning, if necessary. Ladle the broth and pasta into warmed soup bowls and serve immediately.

SERVES 4

500 g/1 lb 2 oz ripe tomatoes, peeled and halved

8 garlic cloves, peeled but left whole

1 Spanish onion, chopped

½ tsp saffron threads, lightly crushed

1 tsp sugar

1 bouquet garni

5-cm/2-inch strip thinly pared lemon rind

600 ml/1 pint vegetable or chicken stock

2 tbsp extra virgin olive oil

280 g/10 oz dried angel hair pasta

salt and pepper

Brown Lentil & Pasta Soup

Place the bacon in a large frying pan together with the onion, garlic and celery. Dry fry for 4–5 minutes, stirring, until the onion is tender and the bacon is just beginning to brown.

Add the pasta to the frying pan and cook, stirring, for 1 minute to coat the pasta in the fat.

Add the lentils and the vegetable stock and bring to the boil. Reduce the heat and leave to simmer for 12–15 minutes, or until the pasta is tender but still firm to the bite.

Remove the frying pan from the heat and stir in the chopped fresh mint. Transfer the soup to warmed soup bowls, garnish with fresh mint sprigs and serve immediately.

SERVES 4

4 rashers streaky bacon, cut into small squares

1 onion, chopped

2 garlic cloves, crushed

2 celery sticks, chopped

50 g/1¾ oz dried farfalline

400 g/14 oz canned brown lentils, drained

1.2 litres/2 pints vegetable stock

2 tbsp chopped fresh mint

fresh mint sprigs, to garnish

Tuscan Bean Soup

Place half the cannellini and half the borlotti beans in a food processor with half the stock and process until smooth. Pour into a large, heavy-based saucepan and add the remaining beans. Stir in enough of the remaining stock to achieve the consistency you like, then bring to the boil.

Add the pasta and return to the boil, then reduce the heat and cook for 15 minutes, or until just tender.

Meanwhile, heat 3 tablespoons of the oil in a small frying pan. Add the garlic and cook, stirring constantly, for 2–3 minutes, or until golden. Stir the garlic into the soup with the parsley.

Season to taste with salt and pepper and ladle into warmed soup bowls. Drizzle with the remaining olive oil to taste and serve immediately.

SERVES 6

300 g/10½ oz canned cannellini
  beans, drained and rinsed
300 g/10½ oz canned borlotti
  beans, drained and rinsed
about 600 ml/1 pint chicken or
  vegetable stock
115 g/4 oz dried conchigliette
4–5 tbsp olive oil
2 garlic cloves, very finely chopped
3 tbsp chopped fresh flat-leaf
  parsley
salt and pepper

Potato & Pesto Soup

To make the pesto, put all of the ingredients in a food processor or blender and process for 2 minutes, or blend by hand using a pestle and mortar.

Heat the oil in a large saucepan and cook the bacon over a medium heat for 4 minutes. Add the butter, potatoes and onions and cook for 12 minutes, stirring constantly.

Add the stock and milk to the saucepan, bring to the boil and simmer for 10 minutes. Add the conchigliette and simmer for a further 3–4 minutes.

Blend in the cream and simmer for 5 minutes. Add the chopped parsley, salt and pepper to taste and 2 tablespoons of the pesto sauce. Transfer the soup to individual serving bowls and serve with Parmesan cheese.

SERVES 4

2 tbsp olive oil

3 rindless, smoked bacon, finely chopped

25 g/1 oz butter

450 g/1 lb floury potatoes, chopped

450 g/1 lb onions, finely chopped

600 ml/1 pint chicken stock

600 ml/1 pint milk

100 g/3½ oz dried conchigliette

150 ml/5 fl oz double cream

2 tbsp chopped parsley

salt and pepper

freshly grated Parmesan cheese, to serve

pesto

55 g/2 oz finely chopped fresh parsley

2 garlic cloves, crushed

55 g/2 oz pine kernels, crushed

2 tbsp chopped fresh basil leaves

55 g/2 oz freshly grated Parmesan cheese

white pepper, to taste

150 ml/5 fl oz olive oil

Tortellini in Broth

Heat the oil in a saucepan. Add the onion and garlic and cook over a low heat, stirring occasionally, for 5 minutes, until softened but not browned. Add the beef, increase the heat to medium and cook, stirring with a wooden spoon to break up the meat, for 8–10 minutes, until evenly browned.

Stir in the herbs, season with salt and pepper, add 125 ml/4 fl oz of the stock and bring to the boil. Lower the heat, cover and simmer for 25 minutes, then remove the lid and cook until all the liquid has evaporated. Remove the pan from the heat, discard the bay leaf and leave to cool.

Roll out the pasta dough on a lightly floured surface to 2–3 mm/ ¹⁄₁₆–⅛ inch thick. Using a 2-cm/¾-inch plain biscuit cutter, stamp out rounds. Place about ¼ teaspoon of the meat mixture in the centre of each round.

Brush the edges of each round with a little beaten egg, then fold them in half to make half moons and press the edges to seal. Wrap a half moon around the tip of your index finger until the corners meet and press together to seal. Repeat with the remaining pasta half moons. Place the filled tortellini on a floured tea towel and leave to dry for 30 minutes.

Bring the remaining stock to the boil in a large saucepan. Add the tortellini, bring back to the boil and cook for 3–4 minutes, until tender but still firm to the bite. Ladle the tortellini and broth into warmed soup bowls and serve immediately.

SERVES 6

3 tbsp olive oil

1 red onion, finely chopped

2 garlic cloves, finely chopped

350 g/12 oz fresh beef mince

1 tsp finely chopped fresh thyme

1 fresh rosemary sprig, finely chopped

1 bay leaf

1.7 litres/3 pints beef stock

2 x quantity Basic Pasta Dough (see page 10)

plain flour, for dusting

1 egg, lightly beaten

salt and pepper

Chicken & Bean Soup

Melt the butter in a large pan over a medium heat. Add the spring onions, garlic, marjoram sprig and diced chicken and cook, stirring frequently, for 5 minutes.

Add the chicken stock, chickpeas and bouquet garni. Season to taste with salt and white pepper.

Bring the soup to the boil over a medium heat. Reduce the heat and simmer for about 2 hours.

Add the diced peppers and pasta to the pan, then simmer for a further 20 minutes.

Ladle the soup into 4 warmed serving bowls and garnish with croûtons. Serve immediately.

SERVES 4

2 tbsp butter

3 spring onions, chopped

2 garlic cloves, crushed

1 fresh marjoram sprig, finely
  chopped

350 g/12 oz chicken breasts, diced

1.2 litres/2 pints chicken stock

350 g/12 oz canned chickpeas,
  drained and rinsed

1 bouquet garni

1 red pepper, diced

1 green pepper, diced

115 g/4 oz dried elbow macaroni

salt and white pepper

croûtons, to serve

Fish Soup with Macaroni

Heat the olive oil in a large, heavy-based saucepan. Add the onions and garlic and cook over a low heat, stirring occasionally, for 5 minutes, or until the onions have softened.

Add the fish stock with the tomatoes and their can juices, herbs, saffron and pasta and season to taste with salt and pepper. Bring to the boil, then cover and simmer for 15 minutes.

Discard any mussels with broken shells or any that refuse to close when tapped. Add the mussels, monkfish and prawns to the saucepan. Re-cover the saucepan and simmer for a further 5–10 minutes, until the mussels have opened, the prawns have changed colour and the fish is opaque and flakes easily. Discard any mussels that remain closed. Ladle the soup into warmed bowls and serve.

SERVES 6

2 tbsp olive oil

2 onions, sliced

1 garlic clove, finely chopped

1 litre/1¾ pints fish stock or water

400 g/14 oz canned chopped tomatoes

¼ tsp herbes de Provence

¼ tsp saffron threads

115 g/4 oz dried macaroni

18 live mussels, scrubbed and debearded

450 g/1 lb monkfish fillet, cut into chunks

225 g/8 oz raw prawns, peeled and deveined, tails left on

salt and pepper

Pasta Salad with Walnuts & Dolcelatte

Bring a large, heavy-based saucepan of lightly salted water to the boil. Add the pasta, return to the boil and cook for 8–10 minutes, or until tender but still firm to the bite. Drain and refresh in a bowl of cold water. Drain again.

Mix the walnut oil, safflower oil and vinegar together in a jug, whisking well, and season to taste with salt and pepper.

Arrange the salad leaves in a large serving bowl. Top with the pasta, dolcelatte cheese and walnuts. Pour the dressing over the salad, toss lightly and serve.

SERVES 4

225 g/8 oz dried farfalle

2 tbsp walnut oil

4 tbsp safflower oil

2 tbsp balsamic vinegar

280 g/10 oz mixed salad leaves

225 g/8 oz dolcelatte cheese, diced

115 g/4 oz walnuts, halved and toasted

salt and pepper

Goat's Cheese, Pear & Walnut Salad with Penne

Bring a large pan of lightly salted water to the boil over a medium heat. Add the pasta and cook for about 8–10 minutes, or until tender, but still firm to the bite. Drain the pasta, refresh under cold running water, drain again and leave to cool.

Put the radicchio and Webbs lettuce into a large salad bowl and mix together well. Top with the pasta, walnuts, pears and rocket.

Mix the lemon juice, oil, garlic and vinegar together in a measuring jug. Pour the mixture over the salad ingredients and toss to coat the salad leaves thoroughly.

Add the tomato wedges, onion slices, grated carrot and diced goat's cheese and, using 2 forks, toss together until well mixed. Leave the salad to chill in the refrigerator for about 1 hour before serving.

SERVES 4

250 g/9 oz dried penne
1 head radicchio, torn into pieces
1 Webbs lettuce, torn into pieces
7 tbsp chopped walnuts
2 ripe pears, cored and diced
115 g/4 oz rocket
2 tbsp lemon juice
5 tbsp olive oil
1 garlic clove, chopped
3 tbsp white wine vinegar
4 tomatoes, cut into wedges
1 small onion, sliced
1 large carrot, grated
250 g/9 oz goat's cheese, diced
salt

Pasta Salad with Chargrilled Peppers

Put the whole peppers on a baking sheet and place under a preheated grill, turning frequently, for 15 minutes, until charred all over. Remove with tongs and place in a bowl. Cover with crumpled kitchen paper and set aside.

Meanwhile, bring a large saucepan of lightly salted water to the boil. Add the pasta, bring back to the boil and cook for 8–10 minutes, until tender but still firm to the bite.

Combine the olive oil, lemon juice, pesto and garlic in a bowl, whisking well to mix. Drain the pasta, add it to the pesto mixture while still hot and toss well. Set aside.

When the peppers are cool enough to handle, peel off the skins, then cut open and remove the seeds. Chop the flesh coarsely and add to the pasta with the basil. Season to taste with salt and pepper and toss well. Serve at room temperature.

SERVES 4

1 red pepper

1 orange pepper

280 g/10 oz dried conchiglie

5 tbsp extra virgin olive oil

2 tbsp lemon juice

2 tbsp pesto

1 garlic clove, crushed

3 tbsp shredded fresh basil leaves

salt and pepper

Warm Pasta Salad

To make the dressing, whisk the olive oil, vinegar, sugar and mustard together in a jug. Season to taste with salt and pepper and stir in the basil.

Bring a large, heavy-based saucepan of lightly salted water to the boil. Add the pasta, bring back to the boil and cook for 8–10 minutes, or until tender but still firm to the bite. Drain and transfer to a salad bowl. Add the dressing and toss well.

Add the tomatoes, spring onions, rocket and cucumber, season to taste with salt and pepper and toss. Sprinkle with the Parmesan cheese and serve warm.

SERVES 4

225 g/8 oz dried farfalle

6 pieces of sun-dried tomato in oil, drained and chopped

4 spring onions, chopped

55 g/2 oz rocket, shredded

½ cucumber, deseeded and diced

2 tbsp freshly grated Parmesan cheese

salt and pepper

dressing

4 tbsp olive oil

1 tbsp white wine vinegar

½ tsp caster sugar

1 tsp Dijon mustard

4 fresh basil leaves, finely shredded

salt and pepper

Pasta & Chicken Medley

To make the dressing, whisk all the ingredients together until smooth.

Bring a large saucepan of lightly salted water to the boil. Add the pasta, bring back to the boil and cook for 8–10 minutes, until tender but still firm to the bite. Drain thoroughly, rinse and drain again. Transfer to a bowl and mix in 1 tablespoon of the dressing while hot; set aside until cold.

Combine the mayonnaise, pesto and soured cream in a bowl, and season to taste.

Add the chicken, celery, grapes, carrot and the mayonnaise mixture to the pasta, and toss thoroughly. Check the seasoning, adding more salt and pepper if necessary.

Arrange the pasta mixture on two plates, garnish with the celery leaves and serve.

SERVES 2

125–150 g/4½–5½ oz dried fusilli

2 tbsp mayonnaise

2 tsp pesto

1 tbsp soured cream or natural fromage frais

175 g/6 oz cooked skinless, boneless chicken, cut into strips

1–2 celery sticks, sliced diagonally

125 g/4½ oz black grapes, halved and deseeded

1 large carrot, cut into strips

salt and pepper

celery leaves, to garnish

dressing

1 tbsp white wine vinegar

3 tbsp extra virgin olive oil

salt and pepper

Rare Beef Pasta Salad

Season the steak to taste with salt and pepper, then grill or pan-fry for 4 minutes on each side. Leave to rest for 5 minutes, then, using a sharp knife, slice the steak thinly across the grain and reserve until required.

Meanwhile, bring a large pan of lightly salted water to the boil over a medium heat. Add the pasta and cook for 8–10 minutes, until tender, but still firm to the bite. Drain thoroughly, refresh in cold water and drain again. Toss the pasta in the oil.

Mix the lime juice, fish sauce and honey together in a small pan and cook over a medium heat for about 2 minutes.

Add the spring onions, cucumber, tomato wedges and mint to the pan, then add the steak and mix well. Season with salt to taste.

Transfer the pasta to a large, warmed serving dish and top with the steak and salad mixture. Serve just warm or leave to cool completely.

SERVES 4

450 g/1 lb rump or sirloin steak in 1 piece

450 g/1 lb dried fusilli

4 tbsp olive oil

2 tbsp lime juice

2 tbsp Thai fish sauce

2 tsp clear honey

4 spring onions, sliced

1 cucumber, peeled and cut into 2.5-cm/1-inch chunks

3 tomatoes, cut into wedges

3 tsp finely chopped fresh mint

salt and pepper

Niçoise Pasta Salad

Bring a large pan of lightly salted water to the boil over a medium heat. Add the pasta and cook for 8–10 minutes, until tender but still firm to the bite. Drain and refresh in cold water.

Bring a small pan of lightly salted water to the boil over a medium heat. Add the green beans and cook for 10–12 minutes, or until tender but still firm to the bite. Drain, refresh in cold water, drain again and reserve.

Put the anchovies in a shallow bowl, pour over the milk and leave to stand for 10 minutes. Meanwhile, tear the lettuces into large pieces. Blanch the tomatoes in boiling water for 1–2 minutes, then drain, skin and roughly chop the flesh. Shell the eggs and cut into quarters. Cut the tuna into large chunks.

Drain the anchovies and the pasta. Put all the salad ingredients into a large bowl and gently mix together.

To make the vinaigrette dressing, beat together all the dressing ingredients and chill in the refrigerator until required. Just before serving, pour the vinaigrette dressing over the salad.

SERVES 4

350 g/12 oz dried conchiglie

115 g/4 oz green beans

50 g/1¾ oz canned anchovy fillets, drained

2 tbsp milk

2 small crisp lettuces

3 large beef tomatoes

4 hard-boiled eggs

225 g/8 oz canned tuna, drained

115 g/4 oz stoned black olives

salt

vinaigrette dressing

3 tbsp extra virgin olive oil

2 tbsp white wine vinegar

1 tsp wholegrain mustard

salt and pepper, to taste

Pasta Salad with Melon & Prawns

Bring a large pan of salted water to the boil. Add the pasta, bring back to the boil and cook for 8–10 minutes, until tender but still firm to the bite. Drain, toss with 1 tablespoon of the olive oil and leave to cool.

Meanwhile, peel and devein the prawns, then place them in a large bowl. Halve both the melons and scoop out the seeds with a spoon. Using a melon baller or teaspoon, scoop out balls of the flesh and add them to the prawns.

Whisk together the remaining olive oil, the vinegar, mustard, sugar, parsley and chopped basil in a small bowl. Season to taste with salt and pepper. Add the cooled pasta to the prawn and melon mixture and toss lightly to mix, then pour in the dressing and toss again. Cover with clingfilm and chill in the refrigerator for 30 minutes.

Make a bed of shredded lettuce on a serving plate. Spoon the pasta salad on top, garnish with basil leaves and serve.

SERVES 6

225 g/8 oz green fusilli

5 tbsp extra virgin olive oil

450 g/1 lb cooked prawns

1 Charentais melon

1 Galia melon

1 tbsp red wine vinegar

1 tsp Dijon mustard

pinch of caster sugar

1 tbsp chopped fresh flat-leaf parsley

1 tbsp chopped fresh basil

1 oakleaf or quattro stagioni lettuce, shredded

salt and pepper

fresh basil leaves, to garnish

Meat & Poultry

Popular classics or irresistible innovations, rich and creamy combinations or hot and spicy dishes: whatever your tastes, there's a perfect pasta dish to fit the bill. There are recipes for made-in-minutes family suppers, as well as more sophisticated pasta dishes that are ideal for informal entertaining. You'll be surprised at the range of meat and poultry featured – not just the perhaps predictable beef and chicken, but also ham, bacon, sausages, pork, lamb, turkey and duck.

Spaghetti Bolognese

Heat the oil in a large frying pan. Add the onion and cook for 3 minutes. Add the garlic, carrot, celery and pancetta or bacon and sauté for 3–4 minutes, or until just beginning to brown.

Add the beef and cook over a high heat for another 3 minutes or until all of the meat is brown. Stir in the tomatoes, oregano and red wine and bring to the boil. Reduce the heat and leave to simmer for about 45 minutes.

Stir in the tomato purée and season to taste with salt and pepper.

Cook the spaghetti in a pan of boiling water for 8–10 minutes, until tender but still firm to the bite. Drain thoroughly.

Transfer the spaghetti to a serving plate and pour over the bolognese sauce. Toss to mix well, garnish with parsley and serve hot

SERVES 4

1 tbsp olive oil

1 onion, finely chopped

2 garlic cloves, chopped

1 carrot, chopped

1 celery stick, chopped

50 g/1¾ oz pancetta or streaky bacon, diced

350 g/12 oz fresh lean beef mince

400 g/14 oz canned chopped tomatoes

2 tsp dried oregano

125 ml/4 fl oz red wine

2 tbsp tomato purée

350 g/12 oz dried spaghetti

salt and pepper

chopped fresh parsley, to garnish

Spaghetti with Meatballs

Place the potato in a small pan, add cold water to cover and a pinch of salt and bring to the boil. Cook for 10–15 minutes, until tender, then drain. Either mash thoroughly with a potato masher or fork or pass through a potato ricer.

Combine the potato, beef, onion, egg and parsley in a bowl and season to taste with salt and pepper. Spread out the flour on a plate. With dampened hands, shape the meat mixture into walnut-sized balls and roll in the flour. Shake off any excess.

Heat the oil in a heavy-based frying pan, add the meatballs and cook over a medium heat, stirring and turning frequently, for 8–10 minutes, until golden all over.

Add the passata and tomato purée and cook for a further 10 minutes, until the sauce is reduced and thickened.

Meanwhile, bring a large saucepan of lightly salted water to the boil. Add the pasta, bring back to the boil and cook for 8–10 minutes, or until tender but still firm to the bite.

Drain well and add to the meatball sauce, tossing well to coat. Transfer to a warmed serving dish, garnish with the basil and Parmesan and serve immediately.

SERVES 6

1 potato, diced

400 g/14 oz fresh beef mince

1 onion, finely chopped

1 egg

4 tbsp chopped fresh flat-leaf parsley

plain flour, for dusting

5 tbsp olive oil

400 ml/14 fl oz passata

2 tbsp tomato purée

400 g/14 oz dried spaghetti

salt and pepper

shredded fresh basil and freshly grated Parmesan cheese, to serve

Spaghetti alla Carbonara

Bring a large, heavy-based saucepan of lightly salted water to the boil. Add the pasta, return to the boil and cook for 8–10 minutes, or until tender but still firm to the bite.

Meanwhile, heat the olive oil in a heavy-based frying pan. Add the pancetta and cook over a medium heat, stirring frequently, for 8–10 minutes.

Beat the eggs with the cream in a small bowl and season to taste with salt and pepper. Drain the pasta and return it to the saucepan. Tip in the contents of the frying pan, then add the egg mixture and half the Parmesan cheese. Stir well, then transfer to a warmed serving dish. Serve immediately, sprinkled with the remaining cheese.

SERVES 4

450 g/1 lb dried spaghetti

1 tbsp olive oil

225 g/8 oz rindless pancetta or streaky bacon, chopped

4 eggs

5 tbsp single cream

2 tbsp freshly grated Parmesan cheese

salt and pepper

Macaroni with Sausage, Pepperoncini & Olives

Heat the oil in a large frying pan over a medium heat. Add the onion and cook for 5 minutes, until softened. Add the garlic and cook for a few seconds, until just beginning to colour. Add the sausage and cook until evenly browned.

Stir in the pepperoncini, tomatoes, oregano and stock. Season to taste with salt and pepper. Bring to the boil, then simmer over a medium heat for 10 minutes, stirring occasionally.

Meanwhile, bring a large saucepan of lightly salted water to the boil. Add the pasta, bring back to the boil and cook for 8–10 minutes, or until tender but still firm to the bite. Drain and transfer to a warmed serving dish.

Add the olives and half the cheese to the sauce, then stir until the cheese has melted.

Pour the sauce over the pasta. Toss well to mix. Sprinkle with the remaining cheese and serve immediately.

SERVES 4

1 tbsp olive oil

1 large onion, finely chopped

2 garlic cloves, very finely chopped

450 g/1 lb pork sausage, peeled and coarsely chopped

3 canned pepperoncini, or other hot red peppers, drained and sliced

400 g/14 oz canned chopped tomatoes

2 tsp dried oregano

125 ml/4 fl oz chicken stock or red wine

450 g/1 lb dried macaroni

12–15 stoned black olives, quartered

75 g/2¾ oz freshly grated cheese, such as Cheddar or Gruyère

salt and pepper

Saffron Linguine

Bring a large, heavy-based saucepan of lightly salted water to the boil. Add the pasta, return to the boil and cook for 8–10 minutes, or until tender but still firm to the bite.

Meanwhile, place the saffron in a separate heavy-based saucepan and add the water. Bring to the boil, then remove from the heat and leave to stand for 5 minutes.

Stir the ham, cream and grated Parmesan cheese into the saffron and return the saucepan to the heat. Season to taste with salt and pepper and heat through gently, stirring constantly, until simmering. Remove the saucepan from the heat and beat in the egg yolks. Drain the pasta and transfer to a warmed serving dish. Add the saffron sauce, toss well and serve immediately.

SERVES 4

350 g/12 oz dried linguine

pinch of saffron threads

2 tbsp water

140 g/5 oz ham, cut into strips

175 ml/6 fl oz double cream

55 g/2 oz freshly grated Parmesan cheese

2 egg yolks

salt and pepper

Pepperoni Pasta

Heat 2 tablespoons of the olive oil in a large, heavy-based frying pan. Add the onion and cook over a low heat, stirring occasionally, for 5 minutes, or until softened. Add the red and orange peppers, tomatoes and their can juices, sun-dried tomato paste and paprika and bring to the boil.

Add the pepperoni and parsley and season to taste with salt and pepper. Stir well, bring to the boil, then reduce the heat and simmer for 10–15 minutes.

Meanwhile, bring a large, heavy-based saucepan of lightly salted water to the boil. Add the pasta, return to the boil and cook for 8–10 minutes, or until tender but still firm to the bite. Drain well and transfer to a warmed serving dish. Add the remaining olive oil and toss. Add the sauce and toss again. Sprinkle with parsley and serve immediately.

SERVES 4

3 tbsp olive oil

1 onion, chopped

1 red pepper, deseeded and diced

1 orange pepper, deseeded and diced

800 g/1 lb 12 oz canned chopped tomatoes

1 tbsp sun-dried tomato paste

1 tsp paprika

225 g/8 oz pepperoni sausage, sliced

2 tbsp chopped fresh flat-leaf parsley, plus extra to garnish

450 g/1 lb dried penne

salt and pepper

Rigatoni with Chorizo & Mushrooms

Heat the oil in a frying pan. Add the onion, garlic and celery and cook over a low heat, stirring occasionally, for 5 minutes, until softened.

Meanwhile, bring a large saucepan of salted water to the boil. Add the pasta, bring back to the boil and cook for 8–10 minutes, until tender but still firm to the bite.

While the pasta is cooking, add the chorizo to the frying pan and cook, stirring occasionally, for 5 minutes, until evenly browned. Add the mushrooms and cook, stirring occasionally, for a further 5 minutes. Stir in the coriander and lime juice and season to taste with salt and pepper.

Drain the pasta and return it to the pan. Add the chorizo and mushroom mixture and toss lightly. Divide among individual warmed plates and serve immediately.

SERVES 4

4 tbsp olive oil

1 red onion, chopped

1 garlic clove, chopped

1 celery stick, sliced

400 g/14 oz dried rigatoni

280 g/10 oz chorizo sausage, sliced

225 g/8 oz chestnut mushrooms, halved

1 tbsp chopped fresh coriander

1 tbsp lime juice

salt and pepper

Linguine with Bacon & Olives

Heat the olive oil in a large frying pan. Add the onions, garlic and bacon and cook over a low heat, stirring occasionally, until the onions are softened. Stir in the mushrooms, anchovies and olives, then season to taste with salt, if necessary, and pepper. Simmer for 5 minutes.

Meanwhile, bring a large, heavy-based saucepan of lightly salted water to the boil. Add the pasta, return to the boil and cook for 8–10 minutes, or until tender but still firm to the bite.

Drain the pasta and transfer to a warmed serving dish. Spoon the sauce on top, toss lightly and sprinkle with the Parmesan cheese. Serve immediately.

SERVES 4

3 tbsp olive oil

2 onions, thinly sliced

2 garlic cloves, finely chopped

175 g/6 oz rindless lean bacon, diced

225 g/8 oz mushrooms, sliced

5 canned anchovy fillets, drained

6 black olives, stoned and halved

450 g/1 lb dried linguine

25 g/1 oz freshly grated Parmesan cheese

salt and pepper

Pasta & Pork in Cream Sauce

To make the red wine sauce, heat the oil in a small heavy-based saucepan, add the onion and cook until transparent. Stir in the tomato purée, red wine and oregano. Heat gently to reduce and set aside.

Pound the slices of pork between 2 sheets of clingfilm until wafer thin, then cut into strips. Heat the oil in a frying pan, add the pork and cook for 5 minutes. Add the mushrooms and cook for a further 2 minutes. Strain and pour over the red wine sauce. Reduce the heat and simmer for 20 minutes.

Meanwhile, bring a large, heavy-based saucepan of lightly salted water to the boil. Add the lemon juice, saffron and orechiette, return to the boil and cook for 8–10 minutes, or until tender but still firm to the bite. Drain the pasta thoroughly, return to the saucepan and keep warm.

Stir the cream into the saucepan with the pork and heat for a few minutes.

Boil the quail eggs for 3 minutes, cool them in cold water and remove the shells.Transfer the pasta to a large, warmed serving plate, top with the pork and the sauce and garnish with the eggs. Serve immediately.

SERVES 4

450 g/1 lb pork fillet, thinly sliced
4 tbsp olive oil
225 g/8 oz button mushrooms, sliced
1 tbsp lemon juice
pinch of saffron threads
350 g/12 oz dried orechiette
4 tbsp double cream
12 quail eggs
salt

red wine sauce

1 tbsp olive oil
1 onion, chopped
1 tbsp tomato purée
200 ml/7 fl oz red wine
1 tsp finely chopped fresh oregano

Farfalle with Gorgonzola & Ham

Pour the crème fraîche into a saucepan, add the mushrooms and season with salt and pepper. Bring to just below the boil, then lower the heat and simmer very gently, stirring occasionally, for 8–10 minutes, until the cream has thickened.

Meanwhile, bring a large pan of salted water to the boil. Add the pasta, bring back to the boil and cook for 8–10 minutes, until tender but still firm to the bite.

Remove the pan of mushrooms from the heat and stir in the Gorgonzola until it has melted. Return the pan to a very low heat and stir in the parsley and ham.

Drain the pasta and add it to the sauce. Toss lightly, then divide among individual warmed plates, garnish with parsley and serve.

SERVES 4

225 ml/8 fl oz crème fraîche

225 g/8 oz chestnut mushrooms, quartered

400 g/14 oz dried farfalle

85 g/3 oz Gorgonzola cheese, crumbled

1 tbsp chopped fresh flat-leaf parsley, plus extra sprigs to garnish

175 g/6 oz cooked ham, diced

salt and pepper

Tagliatelle with Spring Lamb

Using a sharp knife, cut small pockets all over the lamb, then insert a garlic slice and a few rosemary leaves in each one. Heat 2 tablespoons of the olive oil in a large heavy-based frying pan. Add the lamb and cook over a medium heat, turning occasionally, for 25–30 minutes, until tender and cooked to your liking.

Meanwhile, chop the remaining rosemary and place in a mortar. Add the remaining oil and pound with a pestle. Season to taste with salt and pepper and set aside.

Remove the lamb from the heat, cover with foil and leave to stand. Bring a large pan of salted water to the boil. Add the pasta, bring back to the boil and cook for 8–10 minutes, until tender but still firm to the bite.

Meanwhile, melt the butter in another pan. Add the mushrooms and cook over a medium-low heat, stirring occasionally, for 5–8 minutes, until tender.

Drain the pasta, return it to the pan and toss with half the rosemary oil. Uncover the lamb and cut it into slices. Divide the tagliatelle among individual warmed plates, season with pepper and top with the lamb and mushrooms. Drizzle with the remaining rosemary oil, sprinkle with the pecorino and serve immediately.

SERVES 4

750 g/1 lb 10 oz boneless lean lamb
   in a single piece
6 garlic cloves, thinly sliced
6–8 fresh rosemary sprigs
125 ml/4 fl oz olive oil
400 g/14 oz dried tagliatelle
55 g/2 oz butter
175 g/6 oz button mushrooms
salt and pepper
freshly shaved pecorino cheese,
   to serve

Fettuccine with Chicken & Basil Pesto

To make the pesto, put the basil, olive oil, pine kernels, garlic and a generous pinch of salt in a food processor or blender. Process the ingredients until smooth. Scrape the mixture into a bowl and stir in the cheeses.

Heat the vegetable oil in a frying pan over a medium heat. Cook the chicken breasts, turning once, for 8–10 minutes, until the juices are no longer pink. Cut into small cubes.

Meanwhile, bring a large saucepan of lightly salted water to the boil. Add the pasta, bring back to the boil and cook for 8–10 minutes, or until tender but still firm to the bite. Drain and transfer to a warmed serving dish. Add the chicken and pesto, then season with pepper. Toss well to mix.

Garnish with a sprig of basil and serve warm.

SERVES 4

2 tbsp vegetable oil

4 boneless, skinless chicken breasts

350 g/12 oz dried fettuccine

salt and pepper

sprig of fresh basil, to garnish

pesto

100 g/3½ oz shredded fresh basil

125 ml/4 fl oz extra virgin olive oil

3 tbsp pine kernels

3 garlic cloves, crushed

55 g/2 oz freshly grated Parmesan

2 tbsp freshly grated pecorino

salt

Spaghetti with Parsley Chicken

Heat the olive oil in a heavy-based saucepan. Add the lemon rind and cook over a low heat, stirring frequently, for 5 minutes. Stir in the ginger and sugar, season to taste with salt and cook, stirring constantly, for a further 2 minutes. Pour in the chicken stock, bring to the boil, then cook for 5 minutes, or until the liquid has reduced by half.

Meanwhile, bring a large, heavy-based saucepan of lightly salted water to the boil. Add the pasta, return to the boil and cook for 8–10 minutes, or until tender but still firm to the bite.

Melt half the butter in a frying pan. Add the chicken and onion and cook, stirring frequently, for 5 minutes, or until the chicken is light brown all over. Stir in the lemon and ginger mixture and cook for 1 minute. Stir in the parsley leaves and cook, stirring constantly, for a further 3 minutes.

Drain the pasta and transfer to a warmed serving dish, then add the remaining butter and toss well. Add the chicken sauce, toss again and serve.

SERVES 4

1 tbsp olive oil

thinly pared rind of 1 lemon, cut into julienne strips

1 tsp finely chopped fresh ginger

1 tsp sugar

225 ml/8 fl oz chicken stock

250 g/9 oz dried spaghetti

55 g/2 oz butter

225 g/8 oz skinless, boneless chicken breasts, diced

1 red onion, finely chopped

leaves from 2 bunches of flat-leaf parsley

salt

Pappardelle with Chicken & Porcini

Place the porcini in a small bowl, add the hot water and leave to soak for 20 minutes. Meanwhile, place the tomatoes and their can juices in a heavy-based saucepan and break them up with a wooden spoon, then stir in the chilli. Bring to the boil, reduce the heat and simmer, stirring occasionally, for 30 minutes, or until reduced.

Remove the mushrooms from their soaking liquid with a perforated spoon, reserving the liquid. Sieve the liquid through a coffee filter paper or muslin-lined sieve into the tomatoes and simmer for a further 15 minutes.

Meanwhile, heat 2 tablespoons of the olive oil in a heavy-based frying pan. Add the chicken and cook, stirring frequently, until golden brown all over and tender. Stir in the mushrooms and garlic and cook for a further 5 minutes.

While the chicken is cooking, bring a large, heavy-based saucepan of lightly salted water to the boil. Add the pasta, return to the boil and cook for 8–10 minutes, or until tender but still firm to the bite. Drain well, transfer to a warmed serving dish, drizzle with the remaining olive oil and toss lightly. Stir the chicken mixture into the tomato sauce, season to taste with salt and pepper and spoon on top of the pasta. Toss lightly, sprinkle with parsley and serve immediately.

SERVES 4

40 g/1½ oz dried porcini mushrooms

175 ml/6 fl oz hot water

800 g/1 lb 12 oz canned chopped tomatoes

1 fresh red chilli, deseeded and finely chopped

3 tbsp olive oil

350 g/12 oz skinless, boneless chicken, cut into thin strips

2 garlic cloves, finely chopped

350 g/12 oz dried pappardelle

salt and pepper

2 tbsp chopped fresh flat-leaf parsley, to garnish

Penne with Chicken & Rocket

Melt the butter in a heavy-based frying pan. Add the carrots and cook over a medium heat, stirring frequently, for 2 minutes. Add the onion, chicken, mushrooms, wine, chicken stock and garlic and season to taste with salt and pepper. Mix the cornflour and water together in a bowl until a smooth paste forms, then stir in the cream and yogurt. Stir the cornflour mixture into the frying pan with the thyme, cover and leave to simmer for 5 minutes. Place the rocket on top of the chicken, but do not stir in, cover and cook for 5 minutes, or until the chicken is tender.

Sieve the cooking liquid into a clean saucepan, then transfer the chicken and vegetables to a dish and keep warm. Heat the cooking liquid, whisking occasionally, for 10 minutes, or until reduced and thickened.

Meanwhile, bring a large, heavy-based saucepan of lightly salted water to the boil. Add the pasta, return to the boil and cook for 8–10 minutes, or until tender but still firm to the bite. Return the chicken and vegetables to the thickened cooking liquid and stir to coat.

Drain the pasta well, transfer to a warmed serving dish and spoon the chicken and vegetable mixture on top. Garnish with thyme sprigs and serve immediately.

SERVES 4

25 g/1 oz butter

2 carrots, cut into thin batons

1 small onion, finely chopped

225 g/8 oz skinless, boneless
   chicken breast, diced

225 g/8 oz mushrooms, quartered

125 ml/4 fl oz dry white wine

125 ml/4 fl oz chicken stock

2 garlic cloves, finely chopped

2 tbsp cornflour

4 tbsp water

2 tbsp single cream

125 ml/4 fl oz natural yogurt

2 tsp fresh thyme leaves

115 g/4 oz rocket

350 g/12 oz dried penne

salt and pepper

fresh thyme sprigs, to garnish

Pasta with Two Sauces

To make the tomato sauce, heat the oil in a pan over a medium heat. Add the onion and cook until translucent. Add the garlic and cook for 1 minute. Stir in the tomatoes, parsley, oregano, bay leaves, tomato purée and sugar. Season to taste with salt and pepper, bring to the boil and simmer, uncovered, for 15–20 minutes, until reduced by half. Remove the pan from the heat and discard the bay leaves.

To make the chicken sauce, melt the butter in a frying pan over a medium heat. Add the chicken and almonds and cook for 5–6 minutes, or until the chicken is cooked through.

Meanwhile, bring the cream to the boil in a small pan over a low heat and boil for about 10 minutes, until reduced by almost half. Pour the cream over the chicken and almonds, stir and season to taste with salt and pepper. Reserve and keep warm.

Bring a large pan of lightly salted water to the boil over a medium heat. Add the pasta and cook for about 8–10 minutes, or until tender but still firm to the bite. Drain and transfer to a warmed serving dish. Spoon over the tomato sauce and arrange the chicken sauce on top. Garnish with fresh basil leaves and serve.

SERVES 4

250 g/9 oz dried green tagliatelle
salt
fresh basil leaves, to garnish

tomato sauce

2 tbsp olive oil
1 small onion, chopped
1 garlic clove, chopped
400 g/14 oz canned chopped
  tomatoes
2 tbsp chopped fresh parsley
1 tsp dried oregano
2 bay leaves
2 tbsp tomato purée
1 tsp sugar
salt and pepper

chicken sauce

55 g/2 oz unsalted butter
400 g/14 oz boned chicken breasts,
  skinned and cut into thin strips
85 g/3 oz blanched almonds
300 ml/10 fl oz double cream
salt and pepper

Creamy Chicken & Mushroom Tagliatelle

Put the dried mushrooms in a bowl with the hot water. Leave to soak for 30 minutes until softened. Remove, squeezing excess water back into the bowl. Strain the liquid in a fine-meshed sieve and reserve. Slice the soaked mushrooms, discarding the stems.

Heat the oil in a large frying pan over a medium heat. Add the bacon and chicken, then cook for about 3 minutes. Add the dried and fresh mushrooms, the onion and oregano. Cook for 5–7 minutes, until soft. Pour in the stock and the mushroom liquid. Bring to the boil, stirring. Simmer briskly for about 10 minutes, continuing to stir, until reduced. Add the cream and simmer for 5 minutes, stirring, until beginning to thicken. Season with salt and pepper. Remove the pan from the heat and set aside.

Meanwhile, bring a large saucepan of lightly salted water to the boil. Add the pasta, bring back to the boil and cook for 8–10 minutes, or until tender but still firm to the bite. Drain and transfer to a serving dish. Pour the sauce over the pasta. Add half the Parmesan and mix. Sprinkle with parsley and serve with the remaining Parmesan.

SERVES 4

25 g / 1 oz dried shiitake mushrooms

350 ml / 12 fl oz hot water

1 tbsp olive oil

6 bacon rashers, chopped

3 boneless, skinless chicken breasts, sliced into strips

115 g / 4 oz fresh shiitake mushrooms, sliced

1 small onion, finely chopped

1 tsp finely chopped fresh oregano or marjoram

250 ml / 9 fl oz chicken stock

300 ml / 10 fl oz whipping cream

450 g / 1 lb dried tagliatelle

55 g / 2 oz freshly grated Parmesan

salt and pepper

chopped fresh flat-leaf parsley, to garnish

Farfalle with Chicken, Broccoli & Roasted Peppers

Bring a large pan of salted water to the boil. Meanwhile, heat the olive oil and butter in a large frying pan over a medium-low heat. Cook the garlic until just beginning to colour.

Add the diced chicken, raise the heat to medium and cook for 4–5 minutes, until the chicken is no longer pink. Add the chilli flakes and season to taste with salt and pepper. Remove from the heat.

Plunge the broccoli into the boiling water and cook for 2 minutes until tender-crisp. Remove with a perforated spoon and set aside. Bring the water back to the boil. Add the pasta and cook for 8–10 minutes, or until tender but still firm to the bite. Drain and add to the chicken mixture in the pan. Add the broccoli and roasted peppers. Pour in the stock. Simmer briskly over a medium-high heat, stirring frequently, until most of the liquid has been absorbed.

Transfer to warmed dishes and serve.

SERVES 4

4 tbsp olive oil

5 tbsp butter

3 garlic cloves, very finely chopped

450 g/1 lb boneless, skinless chicken breasts, diced

¼ tsp dried chilli flakes

450 g/1 lb small broccoli florets

300 g/10½ oz dried farfalle

175 g/6 oz bottled roasted red peppers, drained and diced

250 ml/9 fl oz chicken stock

salt and pepper

Fettuccine with Chicken & Onion Cream Sauce

Heat the oil and butter with the garlic in a large frying pan over a medium-low heat. Cook the garlic until just beginning to colour. Add the chicken breasts and raise the heat to medium. Cook for 4–5 minutes on each side, until the juices are no longer pink. Season with salt and pepper. Remove from the heat. Remove the chicken breasts, leaving the oil in the pan. Slice the breasts diagonally into thin strips and set aside.

Reheat the oil in the pan. Add the onion and gently cook for 5 minutes until soft. Add the crumbled stock cube and the water. Bring to the boil, then simmer over a medium-low heat for 10 minutes. Stir in the cream, milk, spring onions and Parmesan. Simmer until heated through and slightly thickened.

Meanwhile, bring a large saucepan of lightly salted water to the boil. Add the pasta, bring back to the boil and cook for 8–10 minutes, or until tender but still firm to the bite. Drain and transfer to a warmed serving dish. Layer the chicken slices over the pasta. Pour over the sauce, garnish with parsley and serve.

SERVES 4

1 tbsp olive oil

2 tbsp butter

1 garlic clove, very finely chopped

4 boneless, skinless chicken breasts

1 onion, finely chopped

1 chicken stock cube, crumbled

125 ml/4 fl oz water

300 ml/10 fl oz double cream

175 ml/6 fl oz milk

6 spring onions, green part
   included, sliced diagonally

35 g/1¼ oz freshly grated Parmesan

450 g/1 lb dried fettuccine

salt and pepper

chopped fresh flat-leaf parsley,
   to garnish

Penne with Turkey Meatballs

Put the turkey, garlic and parsley in a bowl and mix well. Stir in the egg and season with salt and pepper. Dust your hands lightly with flour and shape the mixture into walnut-sized balls between your palms. Lightly dust each meatball with flour.

Heat the olive oil in a saucepan. Add the onion, celery and carrot and cook over a low heat, stirring occasionally, for 5 minutes, until softened. Increase the heat to medium, add the meatballs and cook, turning frequently, for 8–10 minutes, until golden brown all over.

Pour in the passata, add the rosemary and bay leaf, season with salt and pepper and bring to the boil. Lower the heat, cover and simmer gently, stirring occasionally, for 40–45 minutes. Remove and discard the herbs.

Shortly before the meatballs are ready, bring a large pan of salted water to the boil. Add the pasta, bring back to the boil and cook for 8–10 minutes, until tender but still firm to the bite. Drain and add to the pan with the meatballs. Stir gently and heat through briefly, then spoon into individual warmed dishes. Sprinkle generously with Parmesan and serve immediately.

SERVES 4

350 g/12 oz fresh turkey mince

1 small garlic clove, finely chopped

2 tbsp finely chopped fresh parsley

1 egg, lightly beaten

plain flour, for dusting

3 tbsp olive oil

1 onion, finely chopped

1 celery stick, finely chopped

1 carrot, finely chopped

400 ml/14 fl oz passata

1 fresh rosemary sprig

1 bay leaf

350 g/12 oz penne

salt and pepper

freshly grated Parmesan cheese,
   to serve

Fettucine with Duck Sauce

Heat half the oil in a heavy-based frying pan. Add the duck legs and cook over a medium heat, turning frequently, for 8–10 minutes, until golden brown all over. Using a perforated spoon, transfer the duck to a large saucepan.

Drain off the oil from the frying pan and wipe with kitchen paper, then add the remaining oil and heat gently. Add the shallot, leek, garlic, celery, carrot and pancetta and cook over a low heat, stirring occasionally, for 10 minutes, until softened. Using a perforated spoon, transfer the mixture to the pan with the duck and stir in the parsley. Add the bay leaf and season with salt and pepper.

Pour in the wine and cook over a high heat, stirring occasionally, until reduced by half. Add the tomatoes, tomato purée and sugar and cook, stirring occasionally, for a further 5 minutes. Pour in just enough water to cover and bring to the boil. Lower the heat, cover and simmer gently for 1 hour, until the duck legs are cooked through and tender.

Remove the saucepan from the heat and transfer the duck legs to a chopping board. Skim off the fat from the surface of the sauce and discard the bay leaf. Remove and discard the skin from the duck and cut the meat off the bones, then dice neatly. Return the duck meat to the pan and keep warm.

Bring a large pan of salted water to the boil. Add the pasta, bring back to the boil and cook for 8–10 minutes, until tender but still firm to the bite. Drain and place in a warmed serving dish. Adjust the seasoning of the sauce, if necessary, then spoon it on top of the pasta. Sprinkle generously with Parmesan and serve immediately.

SERVES 4

4 tbsp olive oil

4 duck legs

1 shallot, finely chopped

1 leek, white part only, finely chopped

1 garlic clove, finely chopped

1 celery stick, finely chopped

1 carrot, finely chopped

4 pancetta or bacon slices, diced

1 tbsp finely chopped fresh flat-leaf parsley

1 bay leaf

5 tbsp dry white wine

400 g/14 oz canned chopped tomatoes

2 tbsp tomato purée

pinch of sugar

450 g/1 lb dried fettucine

salt and pepper

freshly grated Parmesan cheese, to serve

3

Fish & Seafood

Quick to cook, versatile and varied, pasta and fish or seafood must be the perfect partnership. The range of dishes is extensive: economical yet flavour-packed with canned anchovies, fast but elegant with smoked salmon, familiar and new ways with ever-popular prawns and you can even push the boat out with crab and lobster. These recipes are also a great way to encourage children, who are often fussy about fish, to eat it.

Spaghetti alla Puttanesca

Heat the olive oil in a heavy-based frying pan. Add the garlic and cook over a low heat, stirring frequently, for 2 minutes. Add the anchovies and mash them to a pulp with a fork. Add the olives, capers and tomatoes and season to taste with cayenne pepper. Cover and simmer for 25 minutes.

Meanwhile, bring a large, heavy-based saucepan of lightly salted water to the boil. Add the pasta, return to the boil and cook for 8–10 minutes, or until tender but still firm to the bite. Drain well and transfer to a warmed serving dish.

Spoon the anchovy sauce into the dish and toss the pasta, using 2 large forks. Garnish with the chopped parsley, if using, and serve immediately.

SERVES 4

3 tbsp olive oil

2 garlic cloves, finely chopped

10 canned anchovy fillets, drained and chopped

140 g/5 oz black olives, stoned and chopped

1 tbsp capers, drained and rinsed

450 g/1 lb plum tomatoes, peeled, deseeded and chopped

pinch of cayenne pepper

400 g/14 oz dried spaghetti

salt

2 tbsp chopped fresh parsley, to garnish

Penne with Sicilian Sauce

Soak the sultanas in a bowl of warm water for about 20 minutes. Drain the sultanas thoroughly.

Preheat the grill, then cook the tomatoes under the hot grill for 10 minutes. Leave to cool slightly, then once cool enough to handle, peel off the skin and dice the flesh. Place the pine kernels on a baking tray and lightly toast under the grill for 2–3 minutes, or until golden brown.

Place the tomatoes, pine kernels and sultanas in a small saucepan and heat gently. Add the anchovies and tomato purée, and cook the sauce over a low heat for a further 2–3 minutes, or until hot.

Meanwhile, bring a large, heavy-based saucepan of lightly salted water to the boil. Add the pasta, return to the boil and cook for 8–10 minutes, or until tender but still firm to the bite. Drain thoroughly, then transfer the pasta to a serving plate and serve with the Sicilian sauce.

SERVES 4

50 g/1¾ oz sultanas

450 g/1 lb tomatoes, halved

25 g/1 oz pine kernels

50 g/1¾ oz canned anchovies, drained and halved lengthways

2 tbsp tomato purée

350 g/12 oz dried penne

Spinach & Anchovy Pasta

Trim off any tough spinach stalks. Rinse the spinach leaves under cold running water and place them in a large saucepan with only the water that is clinging to them after washing. Cover and cook over a high heat, shaking the saucepan from time to time, until the spinach has wilted, but retains its colour. Drain well, reserve and keep warm.

Bring a large, heavy-based saucepan of lightly salted water to the boil. Add the fettuccine, return to the boil and cook for 8–10 minutes, or until tender but still firm to the bite.

Heat 4 tablespoons of the olive oil in a separate saucepan. Add the pine kernels and fry until golden. Remove the pine kernels from the saucepan and reserve until required.

Add the garlic to the saucepan and fry until golden. Add the anchovies and stir in the spinach. Cook, stirring, for 2–3 minutes, until heated through. Return the pine kernels to the saucepan.

Drain the fettuccine, toss in the remaining olive oil and transfer to a warmed serving dish. Spoon the anchovy and spinach sauce over the fettuccine, toss lightly and serve immediately.

SERVES 4

900 g/2 lb fresh, young spinach leaves

400 g/14 oz dried fettuccine

5 tbsp olive oil

3 tbsp pine kernels

3 garlic cloves, crushed

8 canned anchovy fillets, drained and chopped

salt

Spaghetti with Tuna & Parsley

Bring a large, heavy-based saucepan of lightly salted water to the boil. Add the spaghetti, return to the boil and cook for 8–10 minutes, or until tender but still firm to the bite. Drain the spaghetti in a colander and return to the saucepan. Add the butter, toss thoroughly to coat and keep warm until required.

Flake the tuna into smaller pieces using 2 forks. Place the tuna in a food processor or blender with the anchovies, olive oil and parsley and process until the sauce is smooth. Pour in the crème fraîche and process for a few seconds to blend. Taste the sauce and season with salt and pepper, if necessary.

Warm 6 plates. Shake the saucepan of spaghetti over a medium heat for a few minutes, or until it is thoroughly warmed.

Pour the sauce over the spaghetti and toss quickly, using 2 forks. Serve immediately.

SERVES 6

500 g/1 lb 2 oz dried spaghetti

25 g/1 oz butter

200 g/7 oz canned tuna, drained

55 g/2 oz canned anchovies, drained

250 ml/9 fl oz olive oil

1 large bunch of fresh flat-leaf parsley, coarsely chopped

150 ml/5 fl oz crème fraîche

salt and pepper

Gnocchi with Tuna, Capers & Olives

Bring a large saucepan of lightly salted water to the boil. Add the pasta, bring back to the boil and cook for 8–10 minutes, or until tender but still firm to the bite. Drain and return to the pan.

Heat the olive oil and half the butter in a frying pan over a medium-low heat. Add the garlic and cook for a few seconds until just beginning to colour. Reduce the heat to low. Add the tuna, lemon juice, capers and olives. Stir gently until all the ingredients are heated through.

Transfer the pasta to a warmed serving dish. Pour the tuna mixture over the pasta. Add the parsley and remaining butter. Toss well to mix. Serve immediately.

SERVES 4

350 g/12 oz dried gnocchi

4 tbsp olive oil

4 tbsp butter

3 large garlic cloves, thinly sliced

200 g/7 oz canned tuna, drained and broken into chunks

2 tbsp lemon juice

1 tbsp capers, drained

10–12 black olives, stoned and sliced

salt

2 tbsp chopped fresh flat-leaf parsley, to serve

Springtime Pasta

Fill a bowl with cold water and add the lemon juice. Prepare the artichokes one at a time. Cut off the stems and trim away any tough outer leaves. Cut across the tops of the leaves. Slice in half lengthways and remove the central fibrous chokes, then cut lengthways into 5-mm/¼-inch thick slices. Immediately place the slices in the bowl of acidulated water to prevent discoloration.

Heat 5 tablespoons of the olive oil in a heavy-based frying pan. Drain the artichoke slices and pat dry with kitchen paper. Add them to the frying pan with the shallots, garlic, parsley and mint and cook over a low heat, stirring frequently, for 10–12 minutes, until tender.

Meanwhile, bring a large saucepan of lightly salted water to the boil. Add the pasta, bring back to the boil and cook for 8–10 minutes, until tender but still firm to the bite.

Peel the prawns, cut a slit along the back of each and remove and discard the dark vein. Melt the butter in a small frying pan and add the prawns. Cook, stirring occasionally, for 2–3 minutes, until they have changed colour. Season to taste with salt and pepper.

Drain the pasta and tip it into a bowl. Add the remaining olive oil and toss well. Add the artichoke mixture and the prawns and toss again. Serve immediately.

SERVES 4

2 tbsp lemon juice

4 baby globe artichokes

7 tbsp olive oil

2 shallots, finely chopped

2 garlic cloves, finely chopped

2 tbsp chopped fresh flat-leaf parsley

2 tbsp chopped fresh mint

350 g/12 oz dried rigatoni

12 large uncooked prawns

25 g/1 oz unsalted butter

salt and pepper

Tagliatelle in a Creamy Prawn Sauce

Heat the oil and butter in a saucepan over a medium-low heat. Add the garlic and red pepper. Cook for a few seconds until the garlic is just beginning to colour. Stir in the tomato purée and wine. Cook for 10 minutes, stirring.

Bring a large saucepan of lightly salted water to the boil. Add the pasta, bring back to the boil and cook for 8–10 minutes, or until tender but still firm to the bite. Drain and return to the pan.

Add the prawns to the sauce and raise the heat to medium-high. Cook for 2 minutes, stirring, until the prawns turn pink. Reduce the heat and stir in the cream. Cook for 1 minute, stirring constantly, until thickened. Season with salt and pepper.

Transfer the pasta to a warmed serving dish. Pour the sauce over the pasta. Sprinkle with the parsley. Toss well to mix and serve at once.

SERVES 4

3 tbsp olive oil

3 tbsp butter

4 garlic cloves, very finely chopped

2 tbsp finely diced red pepper

2 tbsp tomato purée

125 ml/4 fl oz dry white wine

450 g/1 lb dried tagliatelle

350 g/12 oz raw peeled prawns

125 ml/4 fl oz double cream

salt and pepper

3 tbsp chopped fresh flat-leaf parsley, to garnish

Linguine with Prawns & Scallops

Peel and devein the prawns, reserving the shells. Melt the butter in a heavy-based frying pan. Add the shallots and cook over a low heat, stirring occasionally, for 5 minutes, or until softened. Add the prawn shells and cook, stirring constantly, for 1 minute. Pour in the vermouth and cook, stirring, for 1 minute. Add the water, bring to the boil, then reduce the heat and simmer for 10 minutes, or until the liquid has reduced by half. Remove the frying pan from the heat.

Bring a large, heavy-based saucepan of lightly salted water to the boil. Add the pasta, return to the boil and cook for 8–10 minutes, or until tender but still firm to the bite.

Meanwhile, heat the olive oil in a separate heavy-based frying pan. Add the scallops and prawns and cook, stirring frequently, for 2 minutes, or until the scallops are opaque and the prawns have changed colour. Strain the prawn-shell stock into the frying pan. Drain the pasta and add to the frying pan with the chives and season to taste with salt and pepper. Toss well over a low heat for 1 minute, then serve.

SERVES 6

450 g/1 lb raw prawns

25 g/1 oz butter

2 shallots, finely chopped

225 ml/8 fl oz dry white vermouth

350 ml/12 fl oz water

450 g/1 lb dried linguine

2 tbsp olive oil

450 g/1 lb prepared scallops,
    thawed if frozen

2 tbsp snipped fresh chives

salt and pepper

Fusilli with Hot Cajun Seafood Sauce

Heat the cream in a large saucepan over a medium heat, stirring constantly. When almost boiling, reduce the heat and add the spring onions, parsley, thyme, pepper, chilli flakes and salt. Simmer for 7–8 minutes, stirring, until thickened. Remove from the heat.

Bring a large saucepan of lightly salted water to the boil. Add the pasta, bring back to the boil and cook for 8–10 minutes, or until tender but still firm to the bite. Drain and return to the pan. Add the cream mixture and the cheeses to the pasta. Toss over a low heat until the cheeses have melted. Transfer to a warmed serving dish.

Heat the oil in a large frying pan over a medium-high heat. Add the prawns and scallops. Cook for 2–3 minutes, until the prawns have just turned pink.

Pour the seafood over the pasta and toss well to mix. Sprinkle with the basil. Serve immediately.

SERVES 4

500 ml/18 fl oz whipping cream

8 spring onions, thinly sliced

55 g/2 oz chopped fresh flat-leaf parsley

1 tbsp chopped fresh thyme

½ tbsp freshly ground black pepper

½–1 tsp dried chilli flakes

1 tsp salt

450 g/1 lb dried fusilli

40 g/1½ oz freshly grated Gruyère

20 g/¾ oz freshly grated Parmesan

2 tbsp olive oil

225 g/8 oz raw peeled prawns

225 g/8 oz scallops, sliced

1 tbsp shredded fresh basil, to garnish

Linguine with Mixed Seafood

Heat the olive oil in a saucepan. Add the shallots, garlic and chilli and cook over a low heat, stirring occasionally, for 5 minutes. Increase the heat to medium, stir in the tomatoes, parsley and sugar and season to taste with salt and pepper. Bring to the boil, then cover and simmer, stirring occasionally, for 15–20 minutes.

Meanwhile, peel and devein the prawns, then set aside. Scrub the mussels and clams under cold running water and pull off the 'beards' from the mussels. Discard any with broken shells or any that refuse to close when tapped.

Pour the wine into a large saucepan with a tight-fitting lid and add the lemon slices, mussels and clams. Cover and cook over a high heat, shaking the pan occasionally, for 5 minutes, until all the shellfish have opened. Using a perforated spoon, transfer the shellfish to a bowl and reserve the cooking liquid.

Discard any mussels and clams that remain closed. Reserve a few for the garnish and remove the remainder from their shells. Strain the cooking liquid through a muslin-lined sieve.

Bring a large saucepan of lightly salted water to the boil. Add the pasta, bring back to the boil and cook for 8–10 minutes, until tender but still firm to the bite.

Meanwhile, stir the strained cooking liquid into the shallot and tomato mixture and bring to the boil, stirring constantly. Add the shelled mussels and clams and the prawns. Taste and adjust the seasoning, if necessary, and heat through gently.

Strain the pasta and return it to the pan. Add the shellfish mixture and toss well. Divide among individual warmed plates, garnish with the reserved mussels and clams and parsley and serve immediately.

SERVES 4–6

2 tbsp olive oil

2 shallots, finely chopped

2 garlic cloves, finely chopped

1 small red chilli, deseeded and finely chopped

200 g/7 oz canned chopped tomatoes

½ bunch fresh flat-leaf parsley, chopped, plus extra sprigs to garnish

pinch of sugar

175 g/6 oz large cooked prawns

450 g/1 lb live mussels

450 g/1 lb live clams

6 tbsp dry white wine

1 lemon, sliced

450 g/1 lb linguine

salt and pepper

Fettuccine with Saffron Mussels

Place the saffron in a small bowl, add the hot water and leave to soak. Discard any mussels with broken shells or any that refuse to close when tapped, then place them in a large, heavy-based saucepan. Add the cold water, cover and cook over a high heat, shaking the saucepan occasionally, for 5 minutes, or until the shells have opened. Remove the mussels with a perforated spoon, reserving the liquid. Discard any that remain closed and remove the remainder from their shells. Strain the cooking liquid through a muslin-lined sieve and reserve.

Heat the oil in a frying pan. Add the onion and cook over a low heat, stirring, for 5 minutes, or until softened. Sprinkle in the flour and cook, stirring, for 1 minute. Remove the pan from the heat. Mix the vermouth and saffron liquid together and gradually whisk into the flour mixture. Return to the heat and simmer, stirring, for 2–3 minutes, or until thickened. Stir in 4 tablespoons of the reserved cooking liquid, the Parmesan, mussels and chives and season to taste with salt and pepper. Simmer for 4 minutes, or until heated through.

Meanwhile, bring a large, heavy-based saucepan of lightly salted water to the boil. Add the pasta, return to the boil and cook for 8–10 minutes, or until tender but still firm to the bite. Drain and transfer to a large, warmed serving dish. Add the mussels and sauce, toss well, garnish with extra snipped chives and serve immediately.

SERVES 4

pinch of saffron threads

175 ml/6 fl oz hot water

1 kg/2 lb 4 oz live mussels, scrubbed and debearded

125 ml/4 fl oz cold water

1 tbsp sunflower oil

1 small onion, finely chopped

2 tbsp plain flour

125 ml/4 fl oz dry white vermouth

4 tbsp freshly grated Parmesan cheese

2 tbsp snipped chives, plus extra to garnish

salt and pepper

350 g/12 oz dried fettuccine

Fusilli with Monkfish & Broccoli

Divide the broccoli florets into tiny sprigs. Bring a saucepan of lightly salted water to the boil, add the broccoli and cook for 2 minutes. Drain and refresh under cold running water.

Heat the olive oil in a large, heavy-based frying pan. Add the monkfish and garlic and season to taste with salt and pepper. Cook, stirring frequently, for 5 minutes, or until the fish is opaque. Pour in the white wine and cream and cook, stirring occasionally, for 5 minutes, or until the fish is cooked through and the sauce has thickened. Stir in the broccoli florets.

Meanwhile, bring a large, heavy-based saucepan of lightly salted water to the boil. Add the pasta, return to the boil and cook for 8–10 minutes, or until tender but still firm to the bite. Drain and tip the pasta into the saucepan with the fish, add the cheese and toss lightly. Serve immediately.

SERVES 4

115 g/4 oz broccoli, divided into florets

3 tbsp olive oil

350 g/12 oz monkfish fillet, skinned and cut into bite-sized pieces

2 garlic cloves, crushed

125 ml/4 fl oz dry white wine

225 ml/8 fl oz double cream

400 g/14 oz dried fusilli

85 g/3 oz Gorgonzola cheese, diced

salt and pepper

Fusilli with Smoked Salmon

Bring a large, heavy-based saucepan of lightly salted water to the boil. Add the pasta, return to the boil and cook for 8–10 minutes, or until tender but still firm to the bite.

Meanwhile, melt the butter in a heavy-based saucepan. Add the onion and cook over a low heat, stirring occasionally, for 5 minutes, or until softened. Add the wine, bring to the boil and continue boiling until reduced by two thirds. Pour in the cream and season to taste with salt and pepper. Bring to the boil, reduce the heat and simmer for 2 minutes, or until slightly thickened. Cut the smoked salmon into squares and stir into the saucepan with the snipped dill and lemon juice to taste.

Drain the pasta and transfer to a warmed serving dish. Add the smoked salmon mixture, toss well, garnish with dill and serve immediately.

SERVES 4

450 g/1 lb dried fusilli

55 g/2 oz unsalted butter

1 small onion, finely chopped

6 tbsp dry white wine

425 ml/15 fl oz double cream

225 g/8 oz smoked salmon

2 tbsp snipped fresh dill, plus extra
  sprigs to garnish

1–2 tbsp lemon juice

salt and pepper

Linguine with Sardines

Wash the sardine fillets and pat dry on kitchen paper. Roughly chop them into large pieces and reserve. Trim the fennel bulb, discard the outer leaves and slice very thinly.

Heat 2 tablespoons of the oil in a large frying pan over a medium-high heat and add the garlic and chillies. Cook for 1 minute, then add the fennel slices. Cook, stirring occasionally, for 4–5 minutes until softened. Reduce the heat, add the sardine pieces and cook for a further 3–4 minutes.

Meanwhile, bring a large pan of lightly salted water to the boil over a medium heat. Add the pasta and cook for 8–10 minutes, or until tender but still firm to the bite. Drain thoroughly and return to the pan.

Add the lemon rind, lemon juice, pine kernels and parsley to the sardines and toss together. Season to taste with salt and pepper. Add to the pasta with the remaining oil and toss together gently. Transfer to a warmed serving dish and serve immediately.

SERVES 4

8 sardines, filleted

1 fennel bulb

4 tbsp olive oil

3 garlic cloves, sliced

1 tsp crushed chillies

350 g / 12 oz dried linguine

½ tsp finely grated lemon rind

1 tbsp lemon juice

2 tbsp pine kernels, toasted

2 tbsp chopped fresh parsley

salt and pepper

Pappardelle with Scallops & Porcini

Put the porcini and hot water in a bowl. Leave to soak for
20 minutes. Strain the mushrooms, reserving the soaking water,
and chop roughly. Line a sieve with two pieces of kitchen paper
and strain the mushroom water into a bowl.

Heat the oil and butter in a large frying pan over a medium heat.
Add the scallops and cook for 2 minutes until just golden. Add
the garlic and mushrooms, then cook for another minute.

Stir in the lemon juice, cream and 125 ml/4 fl oz of the
mushroom water. Bring to the boil, then simmer over a medium
heat for 2–3 minutes, stirring constantly, until the liquid is
reduced by half. Season with salt and pepper. Remove from
the heat.

Bring a large saucepan of lightly salted water to the boil. Add
the pasta, bring back to the boil and cook for 8–10 minutes,
or until tender but still firm to the bite. Drain and transfer to a
warmed serving dish. Briefly reheat the sauce and pour over
the pasta. Sprinkle with the parsley and toss well to mix. Serve
immediately.

SERVES 4

25 g/1 oz dried porcini mushrooms

500 ml/18 fl oz hot water

3 tbsp olive oil

3 tbsp butter

350 g/12 oz scallops, sliced

2 garlic cloves, chopped very finely

2 tbsp lemon juice

250 ml/9 fl oz double cream

350 g/12 oz dried pappardelle

salt and pepper

2 tbsp chopped fresh flat-leaf
  parsley, to serve

Baked Scallops with Pasta in Shells

Preheat the oven to 180°C/350°F/Gas Mark 4. Remove the scallops from their shells. Scrape off the skirt and the black intestinal thread. Reserve the white part (the flesh) and the orange part (the coral or roe). Very carefully ease the flesh and coral from the shell with a short, but very strong knife.

Wash the shells thoroughly and dry them well. Put the shells on a baking tray, sprinkle lightly with 2 tablespoons of the olive oil and set aside.

Meanwhile, bring a large saucepan of lightly salted water to the boil. Add the pasta shells and remaining olive oil and cook for 8–10 minutes, or until tender but still firm to the bite. Drain and spoon about 25 g/1 oz of pasta into each scallop shell.

Put the scallops, fish stock and onion in an ovenproof dish and season to taste with pepper. Cover with foil and bake in the preheated oven for 8 minutes.

Remove the dish from the oven. Remove the foil then use a perforated spoon to transfer the scallops to the shells. Add 1 tbsp of the cooking liquid to each shell, together with a drizzle of lemon juice, a little lemon rind and cream, and top with the Cheddar cheese.

Increase the oven temperature to 230°C/450°F/Gas Mark 8 and return the scallops to the oven for a further 4 minutes.

Serve the scallops in their shells with crusty brown bread.

SERVES 4

12 scallops
3 tbsp olive oil
350 g/12 oz dried conchiglie
150 ml/5 fl oz fresh fish stock
1 onion, chopped
juice and finely grated rind of
   2 lemons
150 ml/5 fl oz double cream
225 g/8 oz grated Cheddar cheese
salt and pepper
crusty brown bread, to serve

Linguine with Clams in Tomato Sauce

Discard any clams with broken shells or any that refuse to close when tapped. Pour the wine into a large, heavy-based saucepan and add the garlic, half the parsley and the clams. Cover and cook over a high heat, shaking the saucepan occasionally, for 5 minutes, or until the shells have opened. Remove the clams with a perforated spoon, reserving the cooking liquid. Discard any that remain closed and remove half of the remainder from their shells. Keep the shelled and unshelled clams in separate covered bowls. Strain the cooking liquid through a muslin-lined sieve and reserve.

Heat the olive oil in a heavy-based saucepan. Add the onion and cook over a low heat for 5 minutes, or until softened. Add the tomatoes, chilli and reserved cooking liquid and season to taste with salt and pepper. Bring to the boil, partially cover the saucepan and simmer for 20 minutes.

Meanwhile, bring a large, heavy-based saucepan of lightly salted water to the boil. Add the pasta, return to the boil and cook for 8–10 minutes, or until tender but still firm to the bite. Drain and transfer to a warmed serving dish.

Stir the shelled clams into the tomato sauce and heat through gently for 2–3 minutes. Pour over the pasta and toss. Garnish with the clams in their shells and remaining parsley. Serve.

SERVES 4

1 kg/2 lb 4 oz live clams, scrubbed

225 ml/8 fl oz dry white wine

2 garlic cloves, coarsely chopped

4 tbsp chopped fresh flat-leaf parsley

2 tbsp olive oil

1 onion, chopped

8 plum tomatoes, peeled, deseeded and chopped

1 fresh red chilli, deseeded and chopped

salt and pepper

350 g/12 oz dried linguine

Spaghetti with Crab

Using a sharp knife, scoop the meat from the crab shell into a bowl. Mix the white and brown meat together lightly and reserve.

Bring a large pan of lightly salted water to the boil over a medium heat. Add the pasta and cook for 8–10 minutes, or until tender but still firm to the bite. Drain thoroughly and return to the pan.

Meanwhile, heat 2 tablespoons of the oil in a frying pan over a low heat. Add the chilli and garlic and cook for 30 seconds, then add the crabmeat, chopped parsley, lemon juice and rind. Cook for 1 minute, until the crab is just heated through.

Add the crab mixture to the pasta with the remaining oil and season to taste with salt and pepper. Toss together thoroughly and transfer to a large, warmed serving dish and garnish with a few lemon wedges. Serve immediately.

SERVES 4

1 dressed crab, about 450 g/
   1 lb including the shell
350 g/12 oz dried spaghetti
6 tbsp extra virgin olive oil
1 fresh red chilli, deseeded and
   finely chopped
2 garlic cloves, finely chopped
3 tbsp chopped fresh parsley
2 tbsp lemon juice
1 tsp finely grated lemon rind
salt and pepper
lemon wedges, to garnish

Farfallini Buttered Lobster

Preheat the oven to 160°C/325°F/Gas Mark 3. Discard the stomach sac, vein and gills from each lobster. Remove the meat from the tail and chop. Crack the claws and legs, remove the meat and chop. Transfer the meat to a bowl and add the lemon juice and lemon rind. Clean the shells and place in the oven to dry out.

Melt 25 g/1 oz of the butter in a frying pan. Add the breadcrumbs and cook for 3 minutes, until crisp and golden brown. Melt the remaining butter in a separate saucepan. Add the lobster meat and heat through gently. Add the brandy and cook for a further 3 minutes, then add the cream and season to taste with salt and pepper.

Meanwhile, bring a large saucepan of lightly salted water to the boil. Add the farfallini and cook for 8–10 minutes, or until tender but still firm to the bite. Drain and spoon the pasta into the clean lobster shells.

Preheat the grill to medium. Spoon the buttered lobster on top of the pasta and sprinkle with a little Parmesan cheese and the breadcrumbs. Grill for 2–3 minutes, or until golden brown. Transfer the lobster shells to a warmed serving dish, garnish with the lemon wedges and dill sprigs and serve immediately.

SERVES 4

2 lobsters (about 700 g/1 lb 9 oz each), split into halves
juice and grated rind of 1 lemon
115 g/4 oz butter
4 tbsp fresh white breadcrumbs
2 tbsp brandy
5 tbsp double cream or crème fraîche
450 g/1 lb dried farfallini
55 g/2 oz freshly grated Parmesan cheese
salt and pepper
lemon wedges and fresh dill sprigs, to garnish

Penne with Squid & Tomatoes

Bring a large, heavy-based saucepan of lightly salted water to the boil. Add the pasta, return to the boil and cook for 3 minutes, then drain and reserve until required. With a sharp knife, cut the squid into strips.

Heat the olive oil in a large saucepan. Add the onions and cook over a low heat, stirring occasionally, for 5 minutes, or until softened. Add the squid and fish stock, bring to the boil and simmer for 3 minutes. Stir in the wine, chopped tomatoes and their can juices, tomato purée, marjoram and bay leaf. Season to taste with salt and pepper. Bring to the boil and cook for 5 minutes, or until slightly reduced.

Add the pasta, return to the boil and simmer for 5–7 minutes, or until tender but still firm to the bite. Remove and discard the bay leaf. Transfer to a warmed serving dish, garnish with the parsley and serve immediately.

SERVES 4

225 g/8 oz dried penne

350 g/12 oz prepared squid

6 tbsp olive oil

2 onions, sliced

225 ml/8 fl oz fish or chicken stock

150 ml/5 fl oz full-bodied red wine

400 g/14 oz canned chopped
    tomatoes

2 tbsp tomato purée

1 tbsp chopped fresh marjoram

1 bay leaf

salt and pepper

2 tbsp chopped fresh parsley,
    to garnish

Vegetarian

Not only do recipes in this chapter feature a wonderful array of vegetables, from artichokes to beans, but they also include great ways with cheese, cream and nuts, as well as fabulous mushroom dishes. Of course, you don't have to be a vegetarian to enjoy these flavoursome pasta sauces and there are dishes to suit all tastes, whether you like your food comforting, piquant, aromatic, succulent or subtle. They are also a great way to ensure a healthy intake of vegetables.

Spaghetti Olio e Aglio

Bring a large, heavy-based saucepan of lightly salted water to the boil. Add the pasta, return to the boil and cook for 8–10 minutes, or until tender but still firm to the bite.

Meanwhile, heat the olive oil in a heavy-based frying pan. Add the garlic and a pinch of salt and cook over a low heat, stirring constantly, for 3–4 minutes, or until golden. Do not allow the garlic to brown or it will taste bitter. Remove the frying pan from the heat.

Drain the pasta and transfer to a warmed serving dish. Pour in the garlic-flavoured olive oil, then add the chopped parsley and season to taste with salt and pepper. Toss well and serve immediately.

SERVES 4

450 g/1 lb dried spaghetti

125 ml/4 fl oz extra virgin olive oil

3 garlic cloves, finely chopped

3 tbsp chopped fresh flat-leaf parsley

salt and pepper

Fettuccine All' Alfredo

Put the butter and 150 ml/5 fl oz of the cream into a large pan and bring the mixture to the boil over a medium heat. Reduce the heat, then simmer gently for 1½ minutes, or until the cream has thickened slightly.

Meanwhile, bring a large pan of lightly salted water to the boil over a medium heat. Add the pasta and cook for 8–10 minutes, or until tender but still firm to the bite. Drain thoroughly and return to the pan, then pour over the cream sauce.

Toss the pasta in the sauce over a low heat, stirring with a wooden spoon, until coated thoroughly.

Add the remaining cream, Parmesan cheese and nutmeg to the pasta mixture and season to taste with salt and pepper. Toss the pasta in the mixture while heating through.

Transfer the pasta mixture to a warmed serving plate and garnish with the fresh parsley sprig. Serve immediately with extra grated Parmesan cheese.

SERVES 4

2 tbsp butter

200 ml/7 fl oz double cream

450 g/1 lb dried fettuccine

85 g/3 oz freshly grated Parmesan cheese, plus extra to serve

pinch of freshly grated nutmeg

salt and pepper

1 fresh flat-leaf parsley sprig, to garnish

Spaghetti with Rocket & Hazelnut Pesto

Put the garlic and hazelnuts in a food processor and process until finely chopped. Add the rocket, Parmesan and olive oil and process until smooth and thoroughly combined. Scrape the pesto into a serving dish, season to taste with salt and pepper and stir in the mascarpone.

Bring a large saucepan of salted water to the boil. Add the pasta, bring back to the boil and cook for 8–10 minutes, until tender but still firm to the bite.

Stir 100–150 ml/3½–5 fl oz of the pasta cooking water into the pesto, mixing well until thoroughly combined. Drain the pasta, add it to the bowl and toss well to coat. Sprinkle with more Parmesan and serve immediately.

SERVES 4

2 garlic cloves

85 g/3 oz hazelnuts

150 g/5 oz rocket, coarse stalks removed

115 g/4 oz freshly grated Parmesan cheese, plus extra to serve

6 tbsp extra virgin olive oil

115 g/4 oz mascarpone cheese

400 g/14 oz spaghetti

salt and pepper

Spaghettini with Tomatoes & Black Olives

Heat the olive oil in a large, heavy-based frying pan. Add the garlic and cook over a low heat for 30 seconds, then add the capers, olives, dried chilli and tomatoes and season to taste with salt. Partially cover the pan and simmer gently for 20 minutes.

Stir in the parsley, partially cover the frying pan again and simmer for a further 10 minutes.

Meanwhile, bring a large, heavy-based saucepan of lightly salted water to the boil. Add the pasta, return to the boil and cook for 5 minutes, or until tender but still firm to the bite. Drain and transfer to a warmed serving dish. Add the tomato and olive sauce and toss well. Sprinkle the Parmesan over the pasta and garnish with extra chopped parsley. Serve immediately.

SERVES 4

1 tbsp olive oil

1 garlic clove, finely chopped

2 tsp bottled capers, drained, rinsed
   and chopped

12 black olives, stoned and chopped

½ dried red chilli, crushed

1.25 kg/2 lb 12 oz canned tomatoes

1 tbsp chopped fresh parsley,
   plus extra to garnish

350 g/12 oz dried spaghettini

2 tbsp freshly grated Parmesan
   cheese

salt

Olive, Pepper & Cherry Tomato Pasta

Bring a large, heavy-based saucepan of lightly salted water to the boil. Add the pasta, return to the boil and cook for 8–10 minutes, or until tender but still firm to the bite. Drain the pasta thoroughly.

Heat the oil and butter in a frying pan until the butter melts. Sauté the garlic for 30 seconds. Add the peppers and cook, stirring constantly, for 3–4 minutes.

Stir in the cherry tomatoes, oregano, wine and olives and cook for 3–4 minutes. Season well with salt and pepper and stir in the rocket until just wilted. Transfer the pasta to a serving dish, spoon over the sauce and garnish with oregano sprigs. Serve.

SERVES 4

225 g/8 oz dried penne

2 tbsp olive oil

25 g/1 oz butter

2 garlic cloves, crushed

1 green pepper, deseeded and thinly sliced

1 yellow pepper, deseeded and thinly sliced

16 cherry tomatoes, halved

1 tbsp chopped fresh oregano, plus extra sprigs to garnish

125 ml/4 fl oz dry white wine

2 tbsp quartered, stoned black olives

75 g/2¾ oz rocket

salt and pepper

Artichoke & Olive Spaghetti

Heat 1 tablespoon of the oil in a large frying pan and gently cook the onion, garlic, lemon juice and aubergines for 4–5 minutes, or until lightly browned.

Pour in the passata, season to taste with salt and pepper and add the sugar and tomato purée. Bring to the boil, reduce the heat and simmer for 20 minutes. Gently stir in the artichoke halves and olives and cook for 5 minutes.

Meanwhile, bring a large, heavy-based saucepan of lightly salted water to the boil. Add the spaghetti, return to the boil and cook for 8–10 minutes, or until just tender but still firm to the bite. Drain well, toss in the remaining olive oil and season to taste with salt and pepper. Transfer the spaghetti to a warmed serving bowl and top with the vegetable sauce. Garnish with basil sprigs and serve with olive bread.

SERVES 4

2 tbsp olive oil

1 large red onion, chopped

2 garlic cloves, crushed

1 tbsp lemon juice

4 baby aubergines, quartered

600 ml/1 pint passata

2 tsp caster sugar

2 tbsp tomato purée

400 g/14 oz canned artichoke hearts, drained and halved

125 g/4½ oz stoned black olives

350 g/12 oz wholemeal dried spaghetti

salt and pepper

fresh basil sprigs, to garnish

olive bread, to serve

Spaghetti alla Norma

Heat 4 tbsp of the olive oil in a large saucepan. Add the tomatoes and garlic, season with salt and pepper, cover and cook over a low heat, stirring occasionally, for 25 minutes.

Meanwhile, heat the remaining oil in a heavy-based frying pan. Add the aubergines and cook, stirring occasionally, for 5 minutes, until evenly golden brown. Remove with a perforated spoon and drain on kitchen paper.

Bring a large pan of salted water to the boil. Add the pasta, bring back to the boil and cook for 8–10 minutes, until tender but still firm to the bite.

Meanwhile, stir the drained aubergines into the pan of tomatoes. Taste and adjust the seasoning, if necessary.

Drain the pasta and place in a warmed serving dish. Add the tomato and aubergine mixture, basil and half the pecorino. Toss well, sprinkle with the remaining pecorino and serve immediately.

SERVES 4

175 ml/6 fl oz olive oil

500 g/1 lb 2 oz plum tomatoes, peeled and chopped

1 garlic clove, chopped

350 g/12 oz aubergines, diced

400 g/14 oz dried spaghetti

½ bunch fresh basil, torn

115 g/4 oz freshly grated pecorino cheese

salt and pepper

Pappardelle with Pumpkin Sauce

Melt the butter in a large, heavy-based saucepan. Add the shallots, sprinkle with a little salt, cover and cook over a very low heat, stirring occasionally, for 30 minutes.

Add the pumpkin pieces and season to taste with nutmeg. Cover and cook over a very low heat, stirring occasionally, for 40 minutes, or until the pumpkin is pulpy. Stir in the cream, Parmesan cheese and parsley and remove the saucepan from the heat.

Meanwhile, bring a large, heavy-based saucepan of lightly salted water to the boil. Add the pasta, return to the boil and cook for 8–10 minutes, or until tender but still firm to the bite. Drain, reserving 2–3 tablespoons of the cooking water.

Add the pasta to the pumpkin mixture and stir in the reserved cooking water if the mixture seems too thick. Cook, stirring, for 1 minute, then transfer to a warmed serving dish and serve immediately with extra grated Parmesan cheese.

SERVES 4

55 g/2 oz butter
6 shallots, very finely chopped
800 g/1 lb 12 oz pumpkin, peeled, deseeded and cut into pieces
pinch of freshly grated nutmeg
200 ml/7 fl oz single cream
4 tbsp freshly grated Parmesan cheese, plus extra to serve
2 tbsp chopped fresh flat-leaf parsley
350 g/12 oz dried pappardelle
salt

Rigatoni with Gorgonzola Sauce

Bring a large, heavy-based saucepan of lightly salted water to the boil. Add the pasta, return to the boil and cook for 8–10 minutes, until tender but still firm to the bite.

Meanwhile, melt the butter in a separate heavy-based saucepan. Add the sage leaves and cook, stirring gently, for 1 minute. Remove and reserve the sage leaves. Add the cheese and cook, stirring constantly, over a low heat until it has melted. Gradually, stir in 175 ml/6 fl oz of the cream and the vermouth. Season to taste with salt and pepper and cook, stirring, until thickened. Add more cream if the sauce seems too thick.

Drain the pasta well and transfer to a warmed serving dish. Add the Gorgonzola sauce, toss well to mix and serve immediately, garnished with the reserved sage leaves.

SERVES 4

400 g/14 oz dried rigatoni

25 g/1 oz unsalted butter

6 fresh sage leaves

200 g/7 oz Gorgonzola cheese, diced

175–225 ml/6–8 fl oz double cream

2 tbsp dry vermouth

salt and pepper

Rigatoni with Peppers & Goat's Cheese

Heat the oil and butter in a large frying pan over a medium heat. Add the onion and cook until soft. Raise the heat to medium-high and add the peppers and garlic. Cook for 12–15 minutes, stirring, until the peppers are tender but not mushy. Season to taste with salt and pepper. Remove from the heat.

Bring a large saucepan of lightly salted water to the boil. Add the pasta, bring back to the boil and cook for 8–10 minutes, or until tender but still firm to the bite. Drain and transfer to a warmed serving dish. Add the goat's cheese and toss to mix.

Briefly reheat the sauce. Add the basil and olives. Pour over the pasta and toss well to mix. Serve immediately.

SERVES 4

2 tbsp olive oil

1 tbsp butter

1 small onion, finely chopped

4 peppers, yellow and red, deseeded and cut into 2-cm/¾-inch squares

3 garlic cloves, thinly sliced

450 g/1 lb dried rigatoni

125 g/4½ oz goat's cheese, crumbled

15 fresh basil leaves, shredded

10 black olives, stoned and sliced

salt and pepper

Penne with Creamy Mushrooms

Melt the butter with the olive oil in a large, heavy-based frying pan. Add the shallots and cook over a low heat, stirring occasionally, for 4–5 minutes, or until softened. Add the mushrooms and cook over a low heat for a further 2 minutes. Season to taste with salt and pepper, sprinkle in the flour and cook, stirring, for 1 minute.

Remove the frying pan from the heat and gradually stir in the cream and port. Return to the heat, add the sun-dried tomatoes and grated nutmeg and cook over a low heat, stirring occasionally, for 8 minutes.

Meanwhile, bring a large, heavy-based saucepan of lightly salted water to the boil. Add the pasta, return to the boil and cook for 8–10 minutes, or until tender but still firm to the bite. Drain the pasta well and add to the mushroom sauce. Cook for 3 minutes, then transfer to a warmed serving dish. Sprinkle with the chopped parsley and serve immediately.

SERVES 4

55 g/2 oz butter

1 tbsp olive oil

6 shallots, sliced

450 g/1 lb chestnut mushrooms, sliced

1 tsp plain flour

150 ml/5 fl oz double cream

2 tbsp port

115 g/4 oz sun-dried tomatoes in oil, drained and chopped

pinch of freshly grated nutmeg

350 g/12 oz dried penne

salt and pepper

2 tbsp chopped fresh flat-leaf parsley, to garnish

Linguine with Wild Mushrooms

Melt the butter in a large, heavy-based frying pan. Add the onion and garlic and cook over a low heat for 5 minutes, or until softened. Add the mushrooms and cook, stirring occasionally, for a further 10 minutes.

Meanwhile, bring a large, heavy-based saucepan of lightly salted water to the boil. Add the pasta, return to the boil and cook for 8–10 minutes, or until tender but still firm to the bite.

Stir the crème fraîche, basil and Parmesan cheese into the mushroom mixture and season to taste with salt and pepper. Cover and heat through gently for 1–2 minutes. Drain the pasta and transfer to a warmed serving dish. Add the mushroom mixture and toss lightly. Garnish with extra basil and serve immediately with extra Parmesan cheese.

SERVES 4

55 g/2 oz butter

1 onion, chopped

1 garlic clove, finely chopped

350 g/12 oz wild mushrooms, sliced

350 g/12 oz dried linguine

300 ml/10 fl oz crème fraîche

2 tbsp shredded fresh basil leaves, plus extra to garnish

4 tbsp freshly grated Parmesan cheese, plus extra to serve

salt and pepper

Linguine with Roasted Garlic & Red Peppers

Place the unpeeled garlic cloves in a shallow, ovenproof dish. Roast in a preheated oven at 200°C/400°F/Gas Mark 6 for 7–10 minutes, until the cloves feel soft.

Put the peppers, tomatoes and oil in a food processor or blender, then purée. Squeeze the garlic flesh into the purée. Add the chilli flakes and thyme. Season to taste with salt and pepper. Blend again, then scrape into a saucepan and set aside.

Bring a large saucepan of lightly salted water to the boil. Add the pasta, bring back to the boil and cook for 8–10 minutes, or until tender but still firm to the bite. Drain and transfer to a warmed serving dish.

Reheat the sauce and pour over the pasta. Toss well to mix and serve immediately.

SERVES 4

6 large garlic cloves, unpeeled

400 g / 14 oz bottled roasted red peppers, drained and sliced

200 g / 7 oz canned chopped tomatoes

3 tbsp olive oil

¼ tsp dried chilli flakes

1 tsp chopped fresh thyme or oregano

350 g / 12 oz dried linguine

salt and pepper

Fusilli with Courgettes & Lemon

Heat the olive oil in a large frying pan over a medium-low heat. Add the onion and cook gently, stirring occasionally, for about 10 minutes, until golden.

Raise the heat to medium-high. Add the garlic, rosemary and parsley. Cook for a few seconds, stirring.

Add the courgettes and lemon rind. Cook for 5–7 minutes, stirring occasionally, until the courgettes are just tender. Season to taste with salt and pepper. Remove from the heat.

Bring a large saucepan of lightly salted water to the boil. Add the pasta, bring back to the boil and cook for 8–10 minutes, or until tender but still firm to the bite. Drain and transfer to a warmed serving dish.

Briefly reheat the courgette sauce. Pour over the pasta and toss well to mix. Sprinkle with the Parmesan and serve immediately.

SERVES 4

6 tbsp olive oil

1 small onion, very thinly sliced

2 garlic cloves, very finely chopped

2 tbsp chopped fresh rosemary

1 tbsp chopped fresh flat-leaf parsley

450 g/1 lb small courgettes, cut into strips measuring 4 cm x 5 mm/1½ x ¼ inches

finely grated rind of 1 lemon

450 g/1 lb dried fusilli

salt and pepper

4 tbsp freshly grated Parmesan, to serve

Vermicelli with Vegetable Ribbons

Bring a large, heavy-based saucepan of lightly salted water to the boil. Add the pasta, return to the boil and cook for 8–10 minutes, or until tender but still firm to the bite.

Meanwhile, cut the courgettes and carrots into very thin strips with a swivel-blade vegetable peeler or a mandolin. Melt the butter with the olive oil in a heavy-based frying pan. Add the carrot strips and garlic and cook over a low heat, stirring occasionally, for 5 minutes. Add the courgette strips and all the herbs and season to taste with salt and pepper.

Drain the pasta and add it to the frying pan. Toss well to mix and cook, stirring occasionally, for 5 minutes. Transfer to a warmed serving dish, add the radicchio, toss well and serve immediately.

SERVES 4

350 g/12 oz dried vermicelli

3 courgettes

3 carrots

25 g/1 oz unsalted butter

1 tbsp olive oil

2 garlic cloves, finely chopped

85 g/3 oz fresh basil, shredded

25 g/1 oz fresh chives, finely snipped

25 g/1 oz fresh flat-leaf parsley, finely chopped

1 small head radicchio, leaves shredded

salt and pepper

Pasta with Green Vegetables

Bring a large, heavy-based saucepan of lightly salted water to the boil. Add the pasta, return to the boil and cook for 8–10 minutes, or until tender but still firm to the bite. Drain the pasta in a colander, return to the saucepan, cover and keep warm.

Steam the broccoli, courgettes, asparagus spears and mangetout over a saucepan of boiling, salted water until just beginning to soften. Remove from the heat and plunge into cold water to prevent further cooking. Drain and reserve. Cook the peas in boiling, salted water for 3 minutes, then drain. Refresh in cold water and drain again.

Place the butter and vegetable stock in a saucepan over a medium heat. Add all the vegetables except for the asparagus spears and toss carefully with a wooden spoon to heat through, taking care not to break them up. Stir in the cream, allow the sauce to heat through and season to taste with salt, pepper and nutmeg.

Transfer the pasta to a warmed serving dish and stir in the chopped parsley. Spoon the sauce over and arrange the asparagus spears on top. Sprinkle with the freshly grated Parmesan and serve hot.

SERVES 4

225 g/8 oz dried fusilli

1 head green broccoli, cut into florets

2 courgettes, sliced

225 g/8 oz asparagus spears, trimmed

125 g/4½ oz mangetout

125 g/4½ oz frozen peas

25 g/1 oz butter

3 tbsp vegetable stock

5 tbsp double cream

large pinch of freshly grated nutmeg

salt and pepper

2 tbsp chopped fresh parsley and 2 tbsp freshly grated Parmesan cheese, to serve

Tagliatelle with Walnuts

Place the breadcrumbs, walnuts, garlic, milk, olive oil and fromage frais in a large mortar and grind to a smooth paste. Alternatively, place the ingredients in a food processor and process until smooth. Stir in the cream to give a thick sauce consistency and season to taste with salt and pepper. Reserve.

Bring a large, heavy-based saucepan of lightly salted water to the boil. Add the pasta, return to the boil and cook for 8–10 minutes, or until tender but still firm to the bite.

Drain the pasta and transfer to a warmed serving dish. Add the walnut sauce and toss thoroughly to coat. Serve immediately.

SERVES 4

25 g/1 oz fresh white breadcrumbs

350 g/12 oz walnut pieces

2 garlic cloves, finely chopped

4 tbsp milk

4 tbsp olive oil

85 g/3 oz fromage frais or cream cheese

150 ml/5 fl oz single cream

350 g/12 oz dried tagliatelle

salt and pepper

Penne with Mixed Beans

Heat the olive oil in a large, heavy-based frying pan. Add the onion, garlic, carrot and celery and cook over a low heat, stirring occasionally, for 5 minutes, or until the onion has softened.

Add the mixed beans, passata and chopped chervil to the frying pan and season the mixture to taste with salt and pepper. Cover and simmer gently for 15 minutes.

Meanwhile, bring a large, heavy-based saucepan of lightly salted water to the boil. Add the pasta, return to the boil and cook for 8–10 minutes, or until tender but still firm to the bite. Drain the pasta and transfer to a warmed serving dish. Add the mixed bean sauce, toss well and serve immediately, garnished with extra chervil.

SERVES 4

1 tbsp olive oil

1 onion, chopped

1 garlic clove, finely chopped

1 carrot, finely chopped

1 celery stick, finely chopped

425 g / 15 oz canned mixed beans, drained and rinsed

225 ml / 8 fl oz passata

1 tbsp chopped fresh chervil, plus extra leaves to garnish

350 g / 12 oz dried penne

salt and pepper

Farfalle with Aubergines

Place the aubergine in a colander, sprinkling each layer with salt, and leave to drain for 30 minutes. Meanwhile, heat 1 tablespoon of the olive oil in a heavy-based saucepan. Add the shallots and garlic and cook over a low heat, stirring occasionally, for 5 minutes, or until softened. Add the tomatoes and their can juices, stir in the sugar and season to taste with salt and pepper. Cover and simmer gently, stirring occasionally, for 30 minutes, or until thickened.

Rinse the aubergine under cold running water, drain well and pat dry with kitchen paper. Heat half the remaining olive oil in a heavy-based frying pan, then add the aubergine in batches, and cook, stirring frequently, until golden brown all over. Remove from the frying pan with a perforated spoon and keep warm while you cook the remaining batches, adding the remaining oil as necessary.

Meanwhile, bring a large, heavy-based saucepan of lightly salted water to the boil. Add the pasta, return to the boil and cook for 8–10 minutes, or until tender but still firm to the bite. Drain the pasta and transfer to a warmed serving dish.

Pour the tomato sauce over the pasta and toss well to mix. Top with the diced aubergine, garnish with fresh basil sprigs and serve.

SERVES 4

1 large or 2 medium aubergines, diced

150 ml/5 fl oz olive oil

4 shallots, chopped

2 garlic cloves, finely chopped

400 g/14 oz canned chopped tomatoes

1 tsp caster sugar

350 g/12 oz dried farfalle

salt and pepper

fresh basil sprigs, to garnish

Filled & Baked

Baked pasta dishes may take a little more time to assemble and cook, but what could be more tempting on a cold winter's evening than layers of lasagne oozing with flavour or a golden brown bubbling pasta bake? This chapter also features a range of ravioli and tortellini recipes using fresh pasta dough. You will be surprised to discover how easy and satisfying filled pasta can be to prepare – and to eat!

Lasagne al Forno

Preheat the oven to 190°C/375°F/Gas Mark 5. Heat the olive oil in a large, heavy-based saucepan. Add the pancetta and cook over a medium heat, stirring occasionally, for 3 minutes, or until the fat begins to run. Add the onion and garlic and cook, stirring occasionally, for 5 minutes, or until softened.

Add the beef and cook, breaking it up with a wooden spoon, until browned all over. Stir in the celery and carrots and cook for 5 minutes. Season to taste with salt and pepper. Add the sugar, oregano and tomatoes and their can juices. Bring to the boil, reduce the heat and simmer for 30 minutes.

Meanwhile, make the cheese sauce. Pour the milk into a saucepan and add the bay leaf, peppercorns, onion and mace. Heat gently to just below boiling point, then remove from the heat, cover and leave to infuse for 10 minutes. Strain the milk into a jug. Melt the butter in a separate saucepan. Sprinkle in the flour and cook over a low heat, stirring constantly, for 1 minute. Remove from the heat and gradually stir in the warm milk. Return to the heat and bring to the boil, stirring. Cook, stirring, until thickened and smooth. Stir in the mustard and both cheeses, then season to taste with salt and pepper.

In a large, rectangular ovenproof dish, make alternate layers of meat sauce, lasagne and Parmesan cheese. Pour the cheese sauce over the layers, covering them completely, and sprinkle with Parmesan cheese. Bake in the preheated oven for 30 minutes, or until golden brown and bubbling. Serve immediately.

SERVES 4

2 tbsp olive oil

55 g/2 oz pancetta or rindless streaky bacon, chopped

1 onion, chopped

1 garlic clove, finely chopped

225 g/8 oz fresh beef mince

2 celery sticks, chopped

2 carrots, chopped

pinch of sugar

½ tsp dried oregano

400 g/14 oz canned chopped tomatoes

225 g/8 oz dried no pre-cook lasagne

115 g/4 oz freshly grated Parmesan cheese, plus extra for sprinkling

salt and pepper

cheese sauce

300 ml/10 fl oz milk

1 bay leaf

6 black peppercorns

slice of onion

blade of mace

25 g/1 oz butter

25 g/1 oz plain flour

2 tsp Dijon mustard

70 g/2½ oz Cheddar cheese, grated

70 g/2½ oz Gruyère cheese, grated

salt and pepper

Beef Lasagne with Ricotta

Heat 100 ml/3½ fl oz of the olive oil with the butter in a large saucepan. Add the bacon, onion, celery and carrot and cook over a low heat, stirring occasionally, for 5 minutes, until softened. Increase the heat to medium, add the beef and cook, turning occasionally, until evenly browned.

Stir in the red wine and tomato paste, season and bring just to the boil. Lower the heat, cover and simmer very gently, stirring occasionally, for 1½ hours, until the beef is tender.

Meanwhile, heat 2 tablespoons of the remaining oil in a frying pan. Add the sausage and cook, turning frequently, for 8–10 minutes. Remove from the pan and remove and discard the skin. Thinly slice the sausage and set aside.

Transfer the beef to a chopping board and dice finely. Return half the beef to the sauce. Mix the remaining beef with 1 egg, 1 tablespoon of the Parmesan and the breadcrumbs in a bowl. Shape the mixture into walnut-sized balls. Heat the remaining olive oil in a frying pan. Cook the meatballs, turning frequently, for 5–8 minutes. Remove with a perforated spoon and set aside.

Pass the ricotta through a sieve into a bowl. Stir in the remaining egg and 4 tablespoons of the remaining Parmesan and season with salt and pepper. Preheat the oven to 180°C/350°F/Gas Mark 4. Grease a rectangular ovenproof dish with butter.

Make layers of lasagne sheets, ricotta mixture, meat sauce, meatballs, sausage and mozzarella in the prepared dish. Finish with a layer of the ricotta mixture and sprinkle with the remaining Parmesan.

Bake the lasagne for 20–25 minutes, or until golden brown. Remove from the oven, garnish with parsley and serve.

SERVES 6

175 ml/6 fl oz olive oil

55 g/2 oz butter, plus extra for greasing

85 g/3 oz bacon or pancetta, diced

1 onion, finely chopped

1 celery stick, finely chopped

1 carrot, finely chopped

350 g/12 oz beef topside in a single piece

5 tbsp red wine

2 tbsp sun-dried tomato paste

200 g/7 oz Italian sausage, such as luganega

2 eggs

115 g/4 oz Parmesan cheese, freshly grated

25 g/1 oz fresh breadcrumbs

350 g/12 oz ricotta cheese

8 sheets no pre-cook lasagne

350 g/12 oz mozzarella cheese, sliced

salt and pepper

fresh chopped parsley, to garnish

Chicken & Spinach Lasagne

To make the tomato sauce, put the tomatoes into a pan and stir in the onion, garlic, wine, tomato purée and oregano. Bring to the boil and simmer for 20 minutes until thick. Season well with salt and pepper.

Preheat the oven to 190°C/375°F/Gas Mark 5. Drain the spinach again and spread it out on kitchen paper to make sure that as much water as possible is removed. Layer the spinach in the base of a large ovenproof baking dish. Sprinkle with ground nutmeg and season to taste with salt and pepper.

Arrange the diced chicken over the spinach and spoon over the tomato sauce. Arrange the sheets of lasagne over the tomato sauce.

Blend the cornflour with a little of the milk to make a paste. Pour the remaining milk into a pan and stir in the paste. Heat, stirring, until the sauce thickens. Season well.

Spoon the sauce over the lasagne and transfer the dish to a baking tray. Sprinkle the grated Parmesan cheese over the sauce and bake in the preheated oven for 25 minutes until golden, then serve.

SERVES 4

350 g/12 oz frozen chopped spinach, thawed and drained

½ tsp freshly grated nutmeg

450 g/1 lb lean, cooked chicken meat, skinned and diced

4 sheets no pre-cook lasagne verde

1½ tbsp cornflour

425 ml/15 fl oz skimmed milk

70 g/2½ oz freshly grated Parmesan cheese

salt and pepper

tomato sauce

400 g/14 oz canned chopped tomatoes

1 onion, chopped finely

1 garlic clove, crushed

150 ml/5 fl oz white wine

3 tbsp tomato purée

1 tsp dried oregano

salt and pepper

Lasagne alla Marinara

Preheat the oven to 190°C/375°F/Gas Mark 5. Melt the butter in a large, heavy-based saucepan. Add the prawns and monkfish and cook over a medium heat for 3–5 minutes, or until the prawns change colour. Transfer the prawns to a small heatproof bowl with a perforated spoon. Add the mushrooms to the saucepan and cook, stirring occasionally, for 5 minutes. Transfer the fish and mushrooms to the bowl.

Stir the fish mixture, with any juices, into the Béchamel Sauce and season to taste with salt and pepper. Layer the tomatoes, chervil, basil, fish mixture and lasagne sheets in a large ovenproof dish, ending with a layer of the fish mixture. Sprinkle evenly with the grated Parmesan cheese.

Bake in the preheated oven for 35 minutes, or until golden brown, then serve immediately.

SERVES 6

15 g/½ oz butter

225 g/8 oz raw prawns, peeled and deveined

450 g/1 lb monkfish fillets, skinned and chopped

225 g/8 oz chestnut mushrooms, chopped

1½ x quantity Béchamel Sauce (see page 184)

400 g/14 oz canned chopped tomatoes

1 tbsp chopped fresh chervil

1 tbsp shredded fresh basil

175 g/6 oz dried no pre-cook lasagne

85 g/3 oz freshly grated Parmesan cheese

salt and pepper

Vegetable Lasagne

For the Béchamel Sauce, pour the milk into a saucepan and add the bay leaf, peppercorns, onion and mace. Heat gently to just below boiling point, then remove from the heat, cover and leave to infuse for 10 minutes. Strain the milk into a jug. Melt the butter in a separate saucepan. Sprinkle in the flour and cook over a low heat, stirring constantly, for 1 minute. Remove from the heat and gradually stir in the warm milk. Return to the heat and bring to the boil, stirring. Cook, stirring, until thickened and smooth. Season to taste with salt and pepper, remove from the heat and set aside.

Preheat the oven to 200°C/400°F/Gas Mark 6. Brush a large ovenproof dish with olive oil. Brush a large griddle pan with olive oil and heat until smoking. Add half the aubergines and cook over a medium heat for 8 minutes, or until golden brown all over. Remove from the griddle pan and drain on kitchen paper. Add the remaining aubergine slices and extra oil, if necessary, and cook for 8 minutes, or until golden brown all over.

Melt the butter in a frying pan and add the garlic, courgettes, parsley and marjoram. Cook over a medium heat, stirring frequently, for 5 minutes, or until the courgettes are golden brown all over. Remove from the frying pan and leave to drain on kitchen paper.

Layer the aubergines, courgettes, mozzarella, passata and lasagne in the dish, seasoning with salt and pepper as you go and finishing with a layer of lasagne. Pour over the Béchamel Sauce, making sure that all the pasta is covered. Sprinkle with the grated Parmesan cheese and bake in the preheated oven for 30–40 minutes, or until golden brown. Serve immediately.

SERVES 4

olive oil, for brushing

2 aubergines, sliced

25 g/1 oz butter

1 garlic clove, finely chopped

4 courgettes, sliced

1 tbsp finely chopped fresh flat-leaf parsley

1 tbsp finely chopped fresh marjoram

225 g/8 oz mozzarella cheese, grated

600 ml/1 pint passata

175 g/6 oz dried no pre-cook lasagne

55 g/2 oz freshly grated Parmesan cheese

salt and pepper

Béchamel Sauce

600 ml/1 pint milk

1 bay leaf

6 black peppercorns

slice of onion

blade of mace

50 g/1¾ oz butter

50 g/1¾ oz plain flour

salt and pepper

Chicken & Wild Mushroom Cannelloni

Preheat the oven to 190°C/375°F/Gas Mark 5. Lightly grease a large ovenproof dish. Heat the olive oil in a heavy-based frying pan. Add the garlic, onion and mushrooms and cook over a low heat, stirring frequently, for 8–10 minutes. Add the chicken mince and prosciutto and cook, stirring frequently, for 12 minutes, or until browned all over. Stir in the Marsala, tomatoes and their can juices, basil and tomato purée and cook for 4 minutes. Season to taste with salt and pepper, then cover and simmer for 30 minutes. Uncover, stir and simmer for 15 minutes.

Meanwhile, bring a large, heavy-based saucepan of lightly salted water to the boil. Add the pasta, return to the boil and cook for 8–10 minutes, or until tender but still firm to the bite. Using a perforated spoon, transfer the cannelloni tubes to a plate and pat dry with kitchen paper.

Using a teaspoon, fill the cannelloni tubes with the chicken and mushroom mixture. Transfer them to the dish. Pour the Béchamel Sauce over them to cover completely and sprinkle with the grated Parmesan cheese.

Bake in the preheated oven for 30 minutes, or until golden brown and bubbling. Serve immediately.

SERVES 4

butter, for greasing
2 tbsp olive oil
2 garlic cloves, crushed
1 large onion, finely chopped
225 g/8 oz wild mushrooms, sliced
350 g/12 oz fresh chicken mince
115 g/4 oz prosciutto, diced
150 ml/5 fl oz Marsala wine
200 g/7 oz canned chopped
    tomatoes
1 tbsp shredded fresh basil leaves
2 tbsp tomato purée
10–12 dried cannelloni tubes
1 x quantity Béchamel Sauce
    (see page 184)
85 g/3 oz freshly grated Parmesan
    cheese
salt and pepper

Cannelloni in Tomato & Red Pepper Sauce

Preheat the oven to 190°C/375°F/Gas Mark 5. Bring a large, heavy-based saucepan of lightly salted water to the boil. Add the pasta, return to the boil and cook for 8–10 minutes, or until tender but still firm to the bite. Transfer the pasta to a plate and pat dry with kitchen paper. Brush a large ovenproof dish with olive oil.

Meanwhile, make the sauce. Heat the oil in a frying pan. Add the shallots and garlic and cook over a low heat for 5 minutes, or until softened. Add the tomatoes, peppers and sun-dried tomato paste and season with salt and pepper. Bring to the boil, then reduce the heat and simmer for 20 minutes. Stir in the basil and pour the sauce into the dish.

While the sauce is cooking, place the broccoli in a saucepan of lightly salted boiling water and cook for 10 minutes, or until tender. Drain and leave to cool slightly, then process to a purée in a food processor. Mix the breadcrumbs, milk and oil together in a large bowl, then stir in the mascarpone cheese, nutmeg, broccoli purée and 4 tablespoons of the pecorino cheese. Season to taste with salt and pepper.

Fill the cannelloni tubes with the broccoli mixture and place them in the dish. Brush with olive oil and sprinkle with the remaining pecorino cheese and almonds. Bake in the preheated oven for 25 minutes, or until golden.

SERVES 4

12 dried cannelloni tubes

450 g/1 lb broccoli, broken into florets

85 g/3 oz fresh breadcrumbs

150 ml/5 fl oz milk

4 tbsp olive oil, plus extra for brushing

225 g/8 oz mascarpone cheese

pinch of grated nutmeg

6 tbsp freshly grated pecorino cheese

2 tbsp flaked almonds

salt and pepper

tomato & red pepper sauce

2 tbsp olive oil

4 shallots, finely chopped

1 garlic clove, finely chopped

600 g/1 lb 5 oz plum tomatoes, skinned, deseeded and chopped

3 red peppers, deseeded and chopped

1 tbsp sun-dried tomato paste

1 tbsp shredded basil leaves

salt and pepper

Vegetable Cannelloni

Preheat the oven to 190°C/375°F/Gas Mark 5. Brush a large ovenproof dish with olive oil. Cut the aubergine into small dice. Heat the oil in a frying pan over a medium heat. Add the aubergine and cook, stirring frequently, for about 2–3 minutes.

Add the spinach, garlic, cumin and mushrooms and reduce the heat. Season to taste with salt and pepper and cook, stirring, for about 2–3 minutes. Spoon the mixture into the cannelloni and put into the dish in a single layer.

To make the sauce, heat the oil in a pan over a medium heat. Add the onion and garlic and cook for 1 minute. Add the tomatoes, sugar and basil and bring to the boil. Reduce the heat and simmer for about 5 minutes. Spoon the sauce over the cannelloni.

Arrange the sliced mozzarella cheese on top of the sauce and bake in the preheated oven for about 30 minutes, or until the cheese is golden brown and bubbling. Serve garnished with lamb's lettuce.

SERVES 4

1 aubergine

125 ml/4 fl oz olive oil, plus extra for brushing

225 g/8 oz spinach

2 garlic cloves, crushed

1 tsp ground cumin

85 g/3 oz mushrooms, chopped

12 dried no pre-cook cannelloni tubes

55 g/2 oz sliced mozzarella cheese

salt and pepper

lamb's lettuce, to garnish

tomato sauce

1 tbsp olive oil

1 onion, chopped

2 garlic cloves, crushed

800 g/1 lb 12 oz canned chopped tomatoes

1 tsp caster sugar

2 tbsp chopped fresh basil

Hot Tomato & Conchiglie Gratin

Put the onion, tomatoes and milk in a large, heavy-based saucepan and bring just to the boil. Add the chillies, garlic, coriander and pasta, season with salt and pepper and cook over a medium heat, stirring frequently, for 2–3 minutes.

Add just enough water to cover and cook, stirring frequently, for 8–10 minutes, until the pasta is tender but still firm to the bite. Meanwhile, preheat the grill.

Spoon the pasta mixture into individual flameproof dishes and sprinkle evenly with the cheese. Place under the grill for 3–4 minutes, until the cheese has melted. Serve immediately.

SERVES 4

1 onion, chopped

400 g/14 oz canned chopped tomatoes

225 ml/8 fl oz milk

1–2 red chillies, deseeded and finely chopped

1 garlic clove, finely chopped

pinch of ground coriander

280 g/10 oz dried conchiglie

85 g/3 oz Gruyère cheese, grated

salt and pepper

Macaroni Cheese & Tomato

Preheat the oven to 190°C/375°F/Gas Mark 5. Grease a deep, ovenproof dish with a little butter.

To make the tomato sauce, heat the oil in a pan over a medium heat. Add the shallot and garlic and cook, stirring constantly, for 1 minute. Add the tomatoes and basil and season to taste with salt and pepper. Cook, stirring, for 10 minutes.

Meanwhile, bring a large pan of lightly salted water to the boil over a medium heat. Add the macaroni and cook for 8–10 minutes, or until tender, but still firm to the bite. Drain well.

Mix the grated Cheddar and Parmesan cheeses together in a small bowl. Spoon one third of the tomato sauce into the base of the prepared dish, then cover with one third of the macaroni and top with one third of the mixed cheeses. Season to taste with salt and pepper. Repeat these layers twice, ending with a layer of the grated cheeses.

Mix the breadcrumbs and basil together and sprinkle evenly over the top. Dot the topping with the butter and cook in the preheated oven for about 25 minutes, or until the topping is golden brown and bubbling. Serve.

SERVES 4

225 g/8 oz dried elbow macaroni

175 g/6 oz freshly grated Cheddar cheese

100 g/3½ oz freshly grated Parmesan cheese

4 tbsp fresh white breadcrumbs

1 tbsp chopped fresh basil

1 tbsp butter or margarine, plus extra for greasing

salt and pepper

tomato sauce

1 tbsp olive oil

1 shallot, chopped finely

2 garlic cloves, crushed

500 g/1 lb 2 oz canned tomatoes

1 tbsp chopped fresh basil

salt and pepper

Pasta & Bean Casserole

Preheat the oven to 180°C/350°F/Gas Mark 4.

Put the beans in a large pan, add water to cover and bring to the boil. Boil the beans rapidly for 20 minutes, then drain them and set aside.

Cook the pasta for 3 minutes in a large saucepan of boiling salted water, adding 1 tablespoon of the olive oil. Drain in a colander and set aside.

Put the beans in a large flameproof casserole, pour in the vegetable stock and stir in the remaining olive oil, the onions, garlic, bay leaves, herbs, red wine and tomato purée.

Bring to the boil, cover the casserole and cook in the preheated oven for 2 hours.

Remove the casserole from the oven and add the reserved pasta, the celery, fennel, mushrooms and tomatoes and season to taste with salt and pepper. Stir in the sugar and sprinkle the breadcrumbs on top. Cover the casserole again, return to the oven and continue cooking for 1 hour. Serve with crusty bread.

SERVES 4

225 g/8 oz dried haricot beans,
  soaked overnight and drained
225 g/8 oz dried penne
6 tbsp olive oil
850 ml/1½ pints vegetable stock
2 large onions, sliced
2 garlic cloves, chopped
2 bay leaves
1 tsp dried oregano
1 tsp dried thyme
5 tbsp red wine
2 tbsp tomato purée
2 celery sticks, sliced
1 fennel bulb, sliced
115 g/4 oz mushrooms, sliced
225 g/8 oz tomatoes, sliced
1 tsp dark muscovado sugar
55 g/2 oz dry white breadcrumbs
salt and pepper
crusty bread, to serve

Pasta Soufflé

Preheat the oven to 190°C/375°F/Gas Mark 5. Heat the olive oil in a large, heavy-based frying pan. Add the onion and cook over a low heat, stirring occasionally, for 5 minutes, or until softened. Add the beef and cook, breaking up the meat with a wooden spoon, until browned. Stir in the garlic, tomatoes and their can juices and tomato purée, then season to taste with salt and pepper. Bring to the boil, reduce the heat and simmer for 20 minutes, then remove the frying pan from the heat and leave to cool slightly.

Meanwhile, bring a large, heavy-based saucepan of lightly salted water to the boil. Add the pasta, return to the boil and cook for 8–10 minutes, or until tender but still firm to the bite. Drain and reserve.

Lightly grease a 1.5-litre/2¾-pint soufflé dish with butter. Beat the egg yolks and add them to the meat sauce, then stir in the pasta. Whisk the egg whites until stiff peaks form, then fold into the sauce. Spoon the mixture into the dish, sprinkle with the grated Parmesan cheese and bake in the preheated oven for 45 minutes, or until well risen and golden brown. Sprinkle with extra grated Parmesan cheese and serve immediately.

SERVES 4

2 tbsp olive oil

1 large onion, chopped

225 g/8 oz fresh beef mince

1 garlic clove, finely chopped

400 g/14 oz canned chopped tomatoes

1 tbsp tomato purée

175 g/6 oz dried elbow macaroni

butter, for greasing

3 eggs, separated

40 g/1½ oz freshly grated Parmesan cheese, plus extra for sprinkling

salt and pepper

Pasticcio

Preheat the oven to 190°C/375°F/Gas Mark 5. Heat the olive oil in a large, heavy-based frying pan. Add the onion and garlic and cook over a low heat, stirring occasionally, for 5 minutes, or until softened. Add the lamb and cook, breaking it up with a wooden spoon, until browned all over. Add the tomato purée and sprinkle in the flour. Cook, stirring, for 1 minute, then stir in the chicken stock. Season to taste with salt and pepper and stir in the cinnamon. Bring to the boil, reduce the heat, cover and cook for 25 minutes.

Meanwhile, bring a large, heavy-based saucepan of lightly salted water to the boil. Add the pasta, return to the boil and cook for 8–10 minutes, or until tender but still firm to the bite.

Drain the pasta and stir into the lamb mixture. Spoon into a large ovenproof dish and arrange the tomato slices on top. Beat together the yogurt and eggs then spoon over the lamb evenly. Bake in the preheated oven for 1 hour. Serve immediately.

SERVES 4

1 tbsp olive oil

1 onion, chopped

2 garlic cloves, finely chopped

450 g/1 lb fresh lamb mince

2 tbsp tomato purée

2 tbsp plain flour

300 ml/10 fl oz chicken stock

1 tsp ground cinnamon

115 g/4 oz dried macaroni

2 beef tomatoes, sliced

300 ml/10 fl oz Greek yogurt

2 eggs, lightly beaten

salt and pepper

Macaroni & Seafood Bake

Preheat the oven to 180°C/350°F/Gas Mark 4. Bring a large saucepan of lightly salted water to the boil. Add the pasta, return to the boil and cook for 8–10 minutes, or until tender but still firm to the bite. Drain and return to the saucepan. Add 25 g/ 1 oz of the butter to the pasta, cover, shake the saucepan and keep warm.

Melt the remaining butter in a separate saucepan. Add the fennel and cook for 3–4 minutes. Stir in the mushrooms and cook for a further 2 minutes. Stir in the prawns, then remove the saucepan from the heat.

Stir the cooked pasta, cayennne pepper and prawn mixture into the Béchamel Sauce.

Grease a large ovenproof dish, then pour the mixture into the dish and spread evenly. Sprinkle over the Parmesan cheese and arrange the tomato slices in a ring around the edge. Brush the tomatoes with olive oil, then sprinkle over the oregano. Bake in the oven for 25 minutes, or until golden brown. Serve immediately.

SERVES 4

350 g/12 oz dried macaroni

85 g/3 oz butter, plus extra for greasing

2 small fennel bulbs, trimmed and thinly sliced

175 g/6 oz mushrooms, thinly sliced

175 g/6 oz cooked peeled prawns

pinch of cayenne pepper

½ x quantity Béchamel Sauce (see page 184)

55 g/2 oz freshly grated Parmesan cheese

2 large tomatoes, halved and sliced

olive oil, for brushing

1 tsp dried oregano

salt and pepper

Baked Tuna & Ricotta Rigatoni

Preheat the oven to 200°C/400°F/Gas Mark 6. Lightly grease a large ovenproof dish with butter. Bring a large, heavy-based saucepan of lightly salted water to the boil. Add the rigatoni, return to the boil and cook for 8–10 minutes, or until just tender but still firm to the bite. Drain the pasta and leave until cool enough to handle.

Meanwhile, mix the tuna and ricotta cheese together in a bowl to form a soft paste. Spoon the mixture into a piping bag and use to fill the rigatoni. Arrange the filled pasta tubes side by side in the prepared dish.

To make the sauce, mix the cream and Parmesan cheese together in a bowl and season to taste with salt and pepper. Spoon the sauce over the rigatoni and top with the sun-dried tomatoes, arranged in a criss-cross pattern. Bake in the preheated oven for 20 minutes. Serve hot straight from the dish.

SERVES 4

butter, for greasing

450 g/1 lb dried rigatoni

200 g/7 oz canned flaked tuna, drained

225 g/8 oz ricotta cheese

125 ml/4 fl oz double cream

225 g/8 oz freshly grated Parmesan cheese

115 g/4 oz sun-dried tomatoes, drained and sliced

salt and pepper

Pumpkin & Ricotta Ravioli

Preheat the oven to 200°C/400°F/Gas Mark 6. Place the unpeeled garlic cloves on a baking sheet and bake for 10 minutes. Meanwhile, put the pumpkin in a steamer set over a pan of boiling water. Cover and steam for 15 minutes, until tender.

Chop the sun-dried tomatoes. Squeeze the garlic cloves out of their skins into a bowl. Add the pumpkin, sun-dried tomatoes, ricotta and rosemary and mash well with a potato masher until thoroughly combined. Season to taste with salt and pepper and leave to cool.

Divide the pasta dough in half and wrap 1 piece in clingfilm. Roll out the other piece on a lightly floured surface to a rectangle 2–3 mm/¹⁄₁₆–⅛ inch thick. Cover with a damp tea towel and roll out the other piece of dough to the same size. Place small mounds, about 1 teaspoon each, of the pumpkin filling in rows 4 cm/1½ inches apart on a sheet of pasta dough. Brush the spaces between the mounds with beaten egg. Lift the second sheet of dough on top and press down firmly between the pockets of filling, pushing out any air bubbles. Using a pasta wheel or sharp knife, cut into squares. Place on a floured tea towel and leave to stand for 1 hour.

Bring a large pan of salted water to the boil. Add the ravioli, bring back to the boil and cook for 3–4 minutes, until tender. Drain, toss with the oil from the sun-dried tomatoes and serve immediately.

SERVES 4

4 garlic cloves

500 g/1 lb 2 oz pumpkin, peeled, deseeded and cut into large chunks

4 sun-dried tomatoes in oil, drained, plus 2 tbsp oil from the jar

115 g/4 oz ricotta cheese

1 tbsp finely chopped fresh rosemary

1 x quantity Basic Pasta Dough (see page 10)

plain flour, for dusting

1 egg, lightly beaten

salt and pepper

Spinach & Ricotta Ravioli

To make the filling, place the spinach in a heavy-based saucepan with just the water clinging to the leaves after washing, then cover and cook over a low heat for 5 minutes, or until wilted. Drain well and squeeze out as much moisture as possible. Leave to cool, then chop finely.

Beat the ricotta cheese until smooth, then stir in the spinach, Parmesan cheese and 1 of the eggs and season to taste with nutmeg and pepper.

Divide the pasta dough in half and wrap 1 piece in clingfilm. Roll out the other piece on a lightly floured surface to a rectangle 2–3 mm/$\frac{1}{16}$–$\frac{1}{8}$ inch thick. Cover with a damp tea towel and roll out the other piece of dough to the same size. Place small mounds, about 1 teaspoon each, of the spinach and ricotta filling in rows 4 cm/1$\frac{1}{2}$ inches apart on a sheet of pasta dough. In a small bowl, lightly beat the remaining egg and use it to brush the spaces between the mounds. Lift the second sheet of dough on top of the first and press down firmly between the pockets of filling, pushing out any air bubbles. Using a pasta wheel or sharp knife cut into squares. Place on a floured tea towel and leave to stand for 1 hour.

Bring a large, heavy-based saucepan of lightly salted water to the boil, add the ravioli, in batches, return to the boil and cook for 5 minutes. Remove with a perforated spoon and drain on kitchen paper. Transfer to a warmed serving dish and serve immediately, sprinkled with Parmesan cheese.

SERVES 4

350 g/12 oz spinach leaves, coarse
  stalks removed
225 g/8 oz ricotta cheese
55 g/2 oz freshly grated Parmesan
  cheese, plus extra to serve
2 eggs
pinch of freshly grated nutmeg
pepper
1 x quantity Spinach Pasta Dough
  (see page 10)
plain flour, for dusting

Garlic Mushroom Ravioli

Heat 25 g/1 oz of the butter in a frying pan. Add the shallots, 1 crushed garlic clove, the mushrooms and celery and cook for 4–5 minutes. Remove the frying pan from the heat, stir in the cheese and season to taste with salt and pepper.

Divide the pasta dough in half and wrap 1 piece in clingfilm. Roll out the other piece on a lightly floured surface to a rectangle 2–3 mm/1/16–1/8 inch thick. Cover with a damp tea towel and roll out the other piece of dough to the same size. Place small mounds, about 1 teaspoon each, of the filling in rows 4 cm/1½ inches apart on a sheet of pasta dough. Brush the spaces between the mounds with the beaten egg. Lift the second sheet of dough on top of the first and press down firmly between the pockets of filling, pushing out any air bubbles. Using a pasta wheel or sharp knife cut into squares. Place on a floured tea towel and leave to stand for 1 hour.

Bring a large, heavy-based saucepan of water to the boil, add the ravioli and cook in batches for 2–3 minutes, or until cooked. Remove with a perforated spoon and drain thoroughly.

Meanwhile, melt the remaining butter in a frying pan. Add the remaining garlic and plenty of pepper and cook for 1–2 minutes. Transfer the ravioli to serving plates and pour over the garlic butter. Garnish with grated pecorino cheese and serve immediately.

SERVES 4

75 g/2¾ oz butter

50 g/1¾ oz shallots, finely chopped

3 garlic cloves, crushed

50 g/1¾ oz mushrooms, wiped and finely chopped

½ celery stick, finely chopped

25 g/1 oz pecorino cheese, finely grated, plus extra to serve

½ x quantity Basic Pasta Dough (see page 10)

plain flour, for dusting

1 egg, lightly beaten

salt and pepper

Creamy Chicken Ravioli

Place the chicken, spinach, prosciutto and shallot in a food processor and process until chopped and blended. Transfer to a bowl, stir in 2 tablespoons of the cheese, the nutmeg and half the egg. Season with salt and pepper.

Divide the pasta dough in half and wrap 1 piece in clingfilm. Roll out the other piece on a lightly floured surface to a rectangle 2–3 mm/¹⁄₁₆–⅛ inch thick. Cover with a damp tea towel and roll out the other piece of dough to the same size. Place small mounds, about 1 teaspoon each, of the filling in rows 4 cm/1½ inches apart on a sheet of pasta dough. Brush the spaces between the mounds with the remaining beaten egg. Lift the second sheet of dough on top of the first and press down firmly between the pockets of filling, pushing out any air bubbles. Using a pasta wheel or sharp knife cut into squares. Place on a floured tea towel and leave to stand for 1 hour.

Bring a large saucepan of lightly salted water to the boil. Add the ravioli in batches, return to the boil and cook for 5 minutes. Remove with a perforated spoon and drain on kitchen paper, then transfer to a warmed dish.

Meanwhile, pour the cream into a frying pan, add the garlic and bring to the boil. Simmer for 1 minute, then add the mushrooms and 2 tablespoons of the remaining cheese. Season to taste and simmer for 3 minutes. Stir in the basil, then pour the sauce over the ravioli. Sprinkle with the remaining cheese, garnish with basil sprigs and serve.

SERVES 4

115 g/4 oz cooked skinless, boneless chicken breast, coarsely chopped

55 g/2 oz cooked spinach

55 g/2 oz prosciutto, coarsely chopped

1 shallot, coarsely chopped

6 tbsp freshly grated pecorino cheese

pinch of freshly grated nutmeg

2 eggs, lightly beaten

1 x quantity Basic Pasta Dough (see page 10)

plain white flour, for dusting

300 ml/10 fl oz double cream

2 garlic cloves, finely chopped

115 g/4 oz chestnut mushrooms, thinly sliced

2 tbsp shredded fresh basil, plus extra sprigs to garnish

salt and pepper

Chicken & Bacon Tortellini

Melt the butter in a large, heavy-based frying pan. Add the chicken, pork and pancetta and cook over a medium heat, stirring frequently, until lightly browned all over. Remove from the frying pan and leave to cool slightly, then transfer to a food processor. Add the mortadella sausage, Parmesan cheese and half the eggs and process until chopped and blended. Scrape the mixture into a large bowl and season to taste with the mixed spice, salt and pepper.

Divide the pasta dough in half and wrap 1 piece in clingfilm. Roll out the other piece to 2–3 mm/¹⁄₁₆–¹⁄₈ inch thick. Cover with a damp tea towel and roll out the other piece of dough to the same thickness. Using a 5-cm/2-inch plain biscuit cutter, stamp out rounds. Place about 1 teaspoon of the prepared filling in the centre of each round. Brush the edges of each round with a little beaten egg, then fold them in half to make half moons and press the edges to seal. Wrap a half moon around the tip of your index finger until the corners meet and press them together to seal. Repeat with the remaining pasta half moons. Place the filled tortellini on a floured tea towel and let stand for 30–60 minutes to dry out slightly before cooking.

Bring a pan of lightly salted water to the boil. Add the tortellini in batches, return to the boil and cook for 10 minutes. Remove with a perforated spoon and drain on kitchen paper, then transfer to a warmed serving dish. Sprinkle the tortellini with the extra grated Parmesan cheese and serve immediately.

SERVES 6

15 g/½ oz butter

115 g/4 oz skinless, boneless chicken breast, diced

115 g/4 oz pork fillet, diced

115 g/4 oz pancetta or rindless streaky bacon, diced

55 g/2 oz mortadella sausage, roughly chopped

115 g/4 oz freshly grated Parmesan cheese, plus extra to serve

2 eggs, lightly beaten

pinch of ground mixed spice

2 x quantity Basic Pasta Dough (see page 10)

plain flour, for dusting

salt and pepper

Beef Ravioli

Heat the oil and half the butter in a large saucepan. Add the braising steak and cook over a medium heat, turning occasionally, for 8–10 minutes, until evenly browned. Remove from the pan.

Lower the heat and add the onion, celery and carrot to the pan. Cook, stirring occasionally, for 5 minutes, until softened. Return the braising steak to the pan, add the wine and cook until reduced by two thirds.

Mix together the beef stock and tomato purée, stir into the pan and season with salt and pepper. Cover and simmer very gently, stirring occasionally, for 3 hours, until the meat is tender and the sauce has thickened.

Remove the braising steak from the pan and leave to cool slightly. Meanwhile, mix together the breadcrumbs and half the Parmesan in a bowl and stir in about half of the sauce (you will not need the remaining sauce). Finely chop the braising steak and stir it into the breadcrumb mixture. Season with salt and pepper, add the nutmeg and cinnamon and stir in the eggs.

Roll out the pasta dough on a lightly floured surface to 2–3 mm/ ⅟₁₆–⅛ inch thick. Using a fluted 5-cm/2-inch biscuit cutter, stamp out rounds. Place about 1 teaspoon of the beef mixture in the centre of each round, brush the edges with water and fold in half to make half moons, pressing the edges to seal. Place on a floured tea towel and leave to stand for 30 minutes.

Bring a large saucepan of salted water to the boil. Add the ravioli, bring back to the boil and cook for 5–8 minutes, until tender. Meanwhile, melt the remaining butter. Drain the ravioli, toss gently in the melted butter and place on a warmed serving dish. Sprinkle with the remaining Parmesan and serve immediately.

SERVES 4

3 tbsp olive oil

70 g/2½ oz butter

350 g/12 oz braising steak, in a single piece

1 red onion, finely chopped

1 celery stick, finely chopped

1 carrot, finely chopped

150 ml/5 fl oz red wine

225 ml/8 fl oz beef stock

1 tbsp tomato purée

55 g/2 oz fresh breadcrumbs

4 tbsp freshly grated Parmesan cheese

pinch of freshly grated nutmeg

pinch of ground cinnamon

2 eggs, lightly beaten

1½ x quantity Basic Pasta Dough (see page 10)

plain flour, for dusting

salt and pepper

Crab Ravioli

Thinly slice the spring onions, keeping the white and green parts separate. Mix the green spring onions, crabmeat, ginger and chilli sauce to taste together in a bowl. Cover with clingfilm and leave to chill until required.

Place the tomatoes in a food processor and process to a purée. Place the garlic, white spring onions and vinegar in a heavy-based saucepan and add the puréed tomatoes. Bring to the boil, stirring frequently, then reduce the heat and simmer gently for 10 minutes. Remove from the heat and reserve.

Divide the pasta dough in half and wrap 1 piece in clingfilm. Roll out the other piece on a lightly floured surface to a rectangle 2–3 mm/$\frac{1}{16}$–$\frac{1}{8}$ inch thick. Cover with a damp tea towel and roll out the other piece of dough to the same size. Place small mounds, about 1 teaspoon each, of the filling in rows 4 cm/1½ inches apart on a sheet of pasta dough. Brush the spaces between the mounds with the remaining beaten egg. Lift the second sheet of dough on top of the first and press down firmly between the pockets of filling, pushing out any air bubbles. Using a pasta wheel or sharp knife cut into squares. Place on a floured tea towel and leave to stand for 1 hour.

Bring a large, heavy-based saucepan of lightly salted water to the boil. Add the ravioli, in batches, return to the boil and cook for 5 minutes. Remove with a perforated spoon and drain on kitchen paper. Meanwhile, gently heat the tomato sauce and whisk in the cream. Place the ravioli on warmed serving plates, pour the sauce over them, garnish with shredded spring onion and serve.

SERVES 4

6 spring onions

350 g/12 oz crabmeat

2 tsp finely chopped fresh ginger

$\frac{1}{8}$–$\frac{1}{4}$ tsp chilli or Tabasco sauce

700 g/1 lb 9 oz tomatoes, peeled, deseeded and roughly chopped

1 garlic clove, finely chopped

1 tbsp white wine vinegar

1 x quantity Basic Pasta Dough (see page 10)

plain flour, for dusting

1 egg, lightly beaten

2 tbsp double cream

salt

shredded spring onion, to garnish